The Atheist's Handbook

Exploring the Philosophy of Non-Belief

Written by August Engels
Published by Cornell-David Publishing House

Index

1. Introduction: The World of Atheism and Non-Belief

The Rich Tapestry of Atheist Thought

As we begin our exploration of atheism and non-belief, it is crucial to appreciate the diverse and multifaceted nature of atheistic thought, which extends far beyond a mere denial of God's existence. Throughout history, this rich tapestry has been woven from numerous philosophical, scientific, and ethical strands, each offering unique perspectives on the nature of the cosmos and our place within it. In this subsection, we shall consider several of these strands, highlighting some of the key figures and ideas that have shaped the contemporary landscape of atheist thought.

Early Skepticism and the Foundations of Secularism

While often associated with the modern era, atheism and religious skepticism can be traced back to the foundations of human thought. In ancient Greece, we find the first glimmers of secularism in the works of the pre-Socratic philosophers, who sought to explain the natural world without recourse to divine interference. Figures like Thales, Democritus, and Epicurus proposed groundbreaking naturalistic theories, which fostered an environment where supernatural explanations could be questioned.

Likewise, in the civilizations of ancient India and China, we encounter schools of thought like the atheistic strands of Hinduism, Jainism, and Confucianism that challenged prevailing religious orthodoxy or rejected the concept of divinity altogether. These early skeptics provided a vital counterpoint to the religious doctrines of their day, and their ideas continue to resonate in the bedrock of modern secularism.

Enlightenment Reason and the Scientific Revolution

Fast forward several centuries, and we arrive at the European Enlightenment, an age defined by its commitment to reason, empiricism, and individual autonomy. This was a time of profound intellectual upheaval, as the authority of the Church was challenged by a torrent of new ideas and discoveries.

Among the thinkers who contributed to this blossoming of atheist thought were David Hume, Baron d'Holbach, and Denis Diderot. Famously, Hume argued for the fallibility of miracles and the limitations of religious knowledge, undercutting the foundations upon which religious belief was based. D'Holbach and Diderot took matters further, espousing outright atheism and advocating for a secular morality based on reason and human well-being.

Meanwhile, the Scientific Revolution was busy transforming our entire understanding of the universe. The pioneering work of Copernicus, Galileo, and Newton demonstrated that the cosmos could be comprehended without the need for a divine architect. This laid the groundwork for later scientists — most notably Charles Darwin — whose discoveries would continue to erode the intellectual foundations of religious belief.

Atheist Existentialism and the Search for Meaning

While atheism's intellectual foundations were being laid in the realms of philosophy and science, another crucial dimension of atheist thought emerged in the 19th and 20th centuries: namely, the struggle to find meaning in a godless universe.

In the works of existentialist philosophers like Friedrich Nietzsche, Jean-Paul Sartre, Albert Camus, and Simone de Beauvoir, atheism was transformed from a mere rejection of the divine to an active embrace of human freedom and responsibility. Rather than lamenting the death of God, these thinkers celebrated the opportunity to create our destiny and forge our values in a world liberated from the shackles of religious dogma.

This positive vision of atheism has carried through to the contemporary era, with figures like Richard Dawkins, Daniel Dennett, A.C. Grayling, and Sam Harris promoting a secular humanism that prizes reason, empathy, and the cultivation of human flourishing.

The Global Landscape of Atheism Today

As we survey the world of atheism and non-belief today, it is important to recognize the global and increasingly interconnected nature of the movement. From the grassroots activism of ex-Muslim atheists advocating for secularism and human rights in their communities to the vibrant secularist traditions of countries like Japan, there is an extraordinary breadth of voices and experiences that make up the atheist tapestry.

Moreover, as technology continues to erode traditional barriers of communication and culture, these diverse voices are only growing louder and more potent, revealing a worldwide community of freethinkers bound together by their commitment to truth, reason, and the humanist ideal.

As you embark upon your journey through the pages of "The Atheist's Handbook," remember that each of these unique perspectives enriches the broader story of atheism and non-belief. By engaging with this rich tapestry, we hope to provide you with not only a comprehensive understanding of atheism but also the tools to think critically, question authority, and live a genuinely examined life.

1.1 A History of Atheism and Non-Belief

In order to understand the landscape of contemporary atheism and non-belief, it is important to first look back at the history of these ideas. While atheism - the disbelief or lack of belief in the existence of God or gods - dates back to ancient civilizations, it has taken on various forms and played different roles throughout history. This section will provide an overview of the timeline of atheism, highlighting some key moments and influential thinkers, in order to set the stage for the rest of the book.

1.1.1 Ancient and Pre-Modern Atheism

Atheism has existed in various guises, albeit sometimes covertly, since the earliest human civilizations. One of the earliest known atheist thinkers was the Indian philosopher Carvaka, who lived in the 6th century BCE. Carvaka rejected the existence of gods and the supernatural, arguing that sensory experience and materialism were the foundations of knowledge.

Ancient Greece was also home to some early atheist thought. The philosopher Epicurus (341–270 BCE) developed a philosophy which has since become commonly associated with atheism, though he did not explicitly reject the existence of gods. Epicureanism posited that the gods, if they existed, played no role in the lives of humans and that the pursuit of pleasure and avoidance of pain were the purpose of life.

During the Roman Empire, many philosophical schools, such as Stoicism and Cynicism, were critical of religious traditions, and figures like the poet Lucretius (99 BCE–55 BCE) openly questioned the existence of gods. However, the coming of Christianity to the Western world largely suppressed atheistic ideas, and it was not until the early modern period that they began to resurface.

1.1.2 The Enlightenment and the Rise of Modern Atheism

The Enlightenment era of the 17th and 18th centuries brought about a renewed interest in science, reason, and skepticism, which in turn led to the emergence of modern atheism. With groundbreaking advancements in fields such as astronomy, physics, and biology, the universe and its workings were beginning to be understood without reference to supernatural or divine entities. Thinkers like David Hume (1711–1776) and Immanuel Kant (1724–1804) offered critiques of traditional religious faith, paving the way for more explicitly atheistic ideas.

In France, the works of philosophers such as Voltaire (1694–1778), Denis Diderot (1713–1784), and Baron d'Holbach (1723–1789) embodied the spirit of skepticism and disbelief. D'Holbach's book, *The System of Nature* (1770), which argued for a purely materialistic view of the universe, was widely condemned and marked a radical departure from the religious zeitgeist.

1.1.3 The 19th Century: Atheism and the Critique of Religion

The 19th century saw a further consolidation of atheistic thought, as well as a proliferation of critiques of religion, which played a large role in shaping the secular worldview. With the rise of critical biblical scholarship and the increasing separation of church and state, religious authority was increasingly called into question.

The German philosopher Friedrich Nietzsche (1844–1900) is, in some ways, the quintessential figure of 19th-century atheism. Nietzsche rejected the claims of both Christianity and traditional morality, declaring (perhaps most famously) that "God is dead." Nietzsche's ideas have continued to resonate with atheists and non-believers, even as his work has been misunderstood and misappropriated by various political movements.

In the latter half of the century, Charles Darwin's groundbreaking work on evolution, as detailed in *The Origin of Species* (1859), struck a significant blow to the traditional religious worldview. Darwin's ideas, along with the emerging fields of geology and paleontology, provided an explanation for the origins of life and the development of species which did not rely on divine creation, further eroding the authority of religious texts.

1.1.4 20th and 21st Century Atheism and Non-Belief

The 20th and 21st century have seen atheism and non-belief continue to grow and diversify, aided by certain cultural and technological shifts. The horrors of the two World Wars, evolving social attitudes, and the increasing secularization of society have driven many to become disillusioned with traditional religious beliefs.

Concurrently, the rise of new forms of digital media, such as the internet and social media platforms, has allowed for the sharing of ideas and the establishment of communities in a manner which was previously impossible. This has led to a rich landscape of contemporary atheism and non-belief, characterized by various subcultures, ideologies, and movements.

In recent decades, several atheist thinkers have gained prominence and sparked public debate. The so-called "New Atheists," a group which includes Richard Dawkins, Sam Harris, Daniel Dennett, and the late Christopher Hitchens, have brought atheism and its criticisms of religion to the forefront of popular culture through their books and other media appearances.

1.1.5 Conclusion

From its roots in ancient civilizations to the present day, the history of atheism and non-belief reveals a rich tapestry of ideas and movements, constantly evolving in response to changing social, political, and intellectual contexts. By examining this history, we are better equipped to understand and engage with the diverse world of contemporary atheism and non-belief as it continues to evolve in the 21st century.

Overview of the Philosophical Arguments for Atheism

In the broad spectrum of atheistic thought, various arguments have been advanced to justify the non-belief in the existence of a deity, or at least to cast doubt on the evidence and reasoning in favor of theism. This chapter provides a comprehensive look at the most prominent arguments for atheism, exploring their historical roots, philosophical underpinnings, and contemporary formulations. We will also juxtapose these atheistic arguments with the popular theological and philosophical arguments for God's existence. This will serve to show that atheism is not based on a shallow rejection of religious ideas, but is rather a well-articulated and thoughtful position supported by robust intellectual tradition.

1.1. The Problem of Evil

One of the most enduring arguments against the existence of an all-powerful, all-knowing, and benevolent deity is the existence of evil, suffering, and injustice in the world. The *problem of evil*, as it is commonly known, dates back to the ancient Greek philosopher Epicurus, as well as early

Christian philosophers such as Saint Augustine and Boethius. The central premise of this argument is that the existence of evil seems to be irreconcilable with the idea of a perfectly good, omnipotent, and omniscient God, whose creation is supposed to be the best world possible.

The problem of evil has been developed in several forms, including the logical problem of evil, which claims that the existence of evil and the existence of an omnipotent, omniscient and benevolent God are logically incompatible. The evidential problem of evil, on the other hand, argues that the extent and variety of evil and suffering in the world provide strong evidence against the existence of such a God. Moreover, the problem of divine hiddenness contends that God's seeming inactivity in the face of evil and human suffering is incompatible with divine love, knowledge, and power.

Theists have put forth various theodicies, or explanations for the existence of evil and suffering, in an attempt to defend their belief in God. These have included the free will defense, the soul-making theodicy, and the greater good theodicy. However, these responses have not been without their own problems and criticisms.

1.2. Logical Positivism, Verificationism, and the Meaninglessness of Religious Language

Another significant argument against the existence of God emerged with the rise of *logical positivism* in the early 20th century. Logical positivists, such as A. J. Ayer and Rudolf Carnap, adhered to the *verification principle*, which posits that a statement is only meaningful if it can be empirically verified or if it is true by definition (i.e., it is analytic). Under this principle, religious language, particularly claims about the existence of God or divine attributes, is rendered meaningless because it cannot be verified empirically or through pure logic.

This argument has been challenged on several grounds, including the fact that the verification principle itself suffers from self-referential problems, as it cannot be proven to be true by either empirical evidence or pure logic. Additionally, some religious claims might be found to have some empirical content (e.g., claims about the efficacy of prayer, the historical veracity of religious texts, and the existence of religious experiences).

1.3. The Presumption of Atheism

Popularized by the philosopher Antony Flew, the *presumption of atheism* argues that atheism should be the default position in the absence of compelling evidence for God's existence. This argument is grounded in the principle that one should not believe in the existence of any entity until there is sufficient evidence to do so. Since the burden of proof lies with the one making the claim, theists must provide sufficient grounds for their belief in God; failing to do so, atheism remains the rational position to adopt.

The presumption of atheism has faced criticisms, primarily on the grounds that it assumes a particular epistemology, namely evidentialism, which assumes that beliefs are only rational if supported by sufficient evidence. Critics argue that belief in God can be justified through other means, such as properly basic beliefs or non-evidential factors like pragmatic considerations.

1.4. Naturalism and the Success of the Natural Sciences

Another key argument put forth by atheists is the success and explanatory power of naturalistic explanations for phenomena previously attributed to supernatural causation. As the natural sciences have advanced, the need to appeal to a divine cause has receded, leading to a shift towards *methodological naturalism*, which assumes that natural explanations are sufficient to account for observed phenomena. By extension, atheists argue that one can embrace *metaphysical naturalism*, which posits that there are no supernatural entities or transcendent beings, including God.

Critics of naturalism argue that there are limits to the explanatory power of naturalistic explanations, and that some phenomena still require a divine explanation. They cite instances such as the origins of the universe and life, the existence of consciousness and moral values, and the parameters of the physical constants as potential evidence for divine intervention.

Conclusion

This chapter has provided an overview of the major philosophical arguments for atheism, which span a wide range of intellectual traditions and disciplines. These arguments represent an ongoing and dynamic conversation between theists and atheists, illustrative of the richness, depth, and complexity of the discourse on a subject of profound importance – the existence, or non-existence, of God. In the course of the following chapters, we will further explore these arguments and delve deeper into the questions that lie at the heart of atheism and non-belief.

2. The History of Atheism: From Ancient Times to the Modern Era

2.1 Atheism in the Ancient World

2.1.1 Ancient Eastern Religions

Before we delve deep into the history of atheism, it is pertinent to understand that the theological landscape in the ancient world was radically different from what it is today. The earliest forms of religious belief were polytheistic, with numerous gods, goddesses, and spirits representing the forces of nature, fertility, and various human emotions.

Many early belief systems, such as Hinduism, Buddhism, Confucianism, and Taoism, evolved in the eastern regions – present-day India, China, and Japan. Although these religions recognized specific gods or deities in their pantheons, some more abstract philosophical themes emerged, such as the absence of a supreme deity or the question of the divine origins of the universe. These concepts influenced thinkers and challenged the roles of gods in southeast Asia and China.

2.1.1.1 Indian Thought

Indian philosophy is famous for its diverse thought, including atheist and agnostic ideas. The **Carvaka School** of thought rejected the idea of a Supreme Being, considering it an anthropocentric construct. Carvakas considered the world to be created by natural forces and events, rather than through the whims of the gods. Instead, they advocated for an empirical and sensory perception of the universe, considering reason and direct experience as primary sources of knowledge.

Another essential development in Indian thought was the emergence of **Jainism** in the 6th century BCE. Mahavira, the spiritual leader of Jainism, developed the concept of *anekantavada* or the multi-sidedness of reality. This principle led to the questioning of the existence and nature of gods, ultimately leading to the emergence of more secular and atheistic ideas in India.

2.1.1.2 Chinese Philosophy

Chinese philosophies such as **Confucianism** and **Taoism** focus more on ethics and equilibrium in the natural world than on theological concerns. Confucianism, founded by Confucius, deals primarily with the moral and ethical principles that govern the proper order of society and individual conduct. Belief in gods or supernatural entities is not a central tenet of Confucianism.

Taoism, however, more directly challenges the notion of theistic belief. Laozi, the founder of Taoism, considered "*The Way*" or "*Tao*" to be the unnameable and ineffable power behind the natural harmony of existence. The Taoist's subtle dismissal of an anthropomorphic divine entity laid the foundations for a more secular outlook in ancient Chinese culture.

2.1.2 Classical Greek and Roman Antiquity

As Western culture evolved, so did its religious beliefs. The influence of Greek and Roman philosophies laid the groundwork for the development of atheistic and agnostic thought in the Western world.

2.1.2.1 Pre-Socratic Philosophers

The pre-Socratics were a group of Greek philosophers who lived around 600 BCE to 400 BCE, prior to the great philosopher **Socrates**. They pondered the unquestioned beliefs in the pantheon of gods and attempted to explain natural phenomena by invoking reason rather than divine intervention.

For example, **Thales of Miletus**, regarded as the first Greek philosopher, attributed the creation and sustenance of the world to natural causes. This shift from supernatural explanations to scientific justification of natural phenomena is essential in understanding the roots of atheism within Western philosophy.

2.1.2.2 Sophists and Socrates

The **Sophists** were a group of philosophers best known for questioning conventional wisdom and promoting critical thinking. Some Sophists openly criticized religious beliefs or adopted a more agnostic stance, such as Protagoras, who stated, "Of the gods, I can know nothing – whether they exist or do not exist – nor what their forms are like."

Socrates, perhaps history's most influential philosopher, promoted the notion of an inner moral compass, the *daimonion* or "inner divine sign." While not specifically atheist or agnostic, Socrates' emphasis on an individual's innate sense of right and wrong formed the basis for later philosophies that centered on ethics without the need for divine intervention.

2.1.2.3 Epicureanism and Stoicism

One of the most essential and long-lasting philosophical systems to develop during this period was **Epicureanism**.

Founded by Epicurus, the philosophy centered on the pursuit of pleasure and freedom from suffering – specifically, through the embrace of reason, knowledge, and materialism. With regard to divinity, Epicurus held that gods might exist, but they did not interfere in human affairs.

Stoicism, a parallel philosophical system founded by Zeno of Citium, emphasized cultivating inner resilience, self-control, and wisdom as the key to happiness. The Stoic concept of god was that of an eternal, rational, and impersonal force permeating the universe. While not explicitly atheistic, Stoicism implied that gods did not play an active role in human life, thereby diminishing the importance of religious beliefs.

2.1.3 The Emergence of Christianity and the Decline of Atheism in the Western World

With the rise of Christianity and its eventual dominance over the Western world, there was a decline in the influence of atheistic and agnostic philosophies. Criticism of conventional religious beliefs became a dangerous enterprise, and those who openly questioned Christianity faced harsh consequences such as persecution, torture, and death.

However, the decline of atheism during this period does not mean that nonbelievers disappeared completely – rather, their voices were muted, and their writings suppressed. It wasn't until the Renaissance and the Enlightenment that the seeds of atheistic thought began to flourish once more.

2.1 Ancient Roots of Atheism: Greece, India, and China

2.1.1 Atheism in Ancient Greece

While people tend to believe that atheism is a modern phenomenon, its origins can be traced back to the ancient civilizations. In the Western world, the foundations of atheism can be found in the philosophies of Ancient Greece.

The concept of atheism as we understand it today has evolved throughout history, and in ancient Greece, the term "atheos" referred to those who were without the belief in gods or denied their existence. Several pre-Socratic philosophers questioned the existence of gods and posed alternative explanations for the universe's creation and existence.

Democritus, a pre-Socratic philosopher, and his mentor Leucippus were among the first materialists in Western philosophy. They postulated that the cosmos was composed of indivisible elements called atoms that moved in a void. Their ideas further suggested that gods could not logically alter the motion of these atoms, implying that gods either did not exist or were unnecessary for our understanding of the universe.

Likewise, another pre-Socratic philosopher, Xenophanes of Colophon, criticized the anthropomorphic nature of the gods and argued that if animals could create gods, they would reflect the animal's appearance. He noted the contradictions between the various gods people believed in and their inability to prevent disasters and natural phenomena.

When it comes to classical Greek philosophy, we can't ignore the atomist philosopher, Epicurus. He questioned the existence and nature of gods, and his teachings gave birth to the famous Epicurean paradox:

Is God willing to prevent evil but not able? Then
he is not omnipotent.

Is he able but not willing? Then he is malevolent.

Is he both able and willing? Then whence cometh
evil?

Is he neither able nor willing? Then why call him
God?

Even the famous philosopher Plato, in his dialogues,
occasionally made Socrates question the existence of gods,
and portray them as irrelevant to the attainment of wisdom
and morality.

2.1.2 Atheism in Ancient India

While Greek philosophers were advocating skepticism and
critical thinking, similar ideas were taking root in ancient
India. The Indian subcontinent is known for its religious
diversity and the development of numerous philosophies and
schools of thought. The Carvaka or Lokayata school is one
such example of a materialistic and atheistic philosophy that
developed in ancient India.

The Carvaka school rejected the idea of an afterlife, karma,
and the existence of otherworldly beings. They refused to
accept the authority of the Vedas (sacred texts) and upheld
the importance of direct perception and empirical evidence
over faith or belief in gods. The Carvaka school showed that
the Indian subcontinent was a fertile ground for the
exploration of non-belief and ancient atheism.

2.1.3 Atheism in Ancient China

Chinese philosophy has been shaped by various schools of thought, which have often intertwined with one another throughout history. Among these philosophical schools, Confucianism and Daoism (or Taoism) emerged as influential systems of thought that did not rely on the existence of deities or supernatural beings. How traditional Chinese religions handle the topic of gods is complex, and sometimes they can be seen as more of allegories or principles than divine beings.

Although many people would not consider Confucianism and Daoism strictly atheistic or agnostic as they recognize spirits, the essence of these philosophical systems is arguably humanistic, and their teachings focus mostly on practical and ethical issues of human relations rather than supernatural beings with divine powers.

Despite this, another school of thought that developed during the Warring States Period (476-221 BCE), called Mohism, actively opposed the worship of gods and spirits. Mohism's teachings advocated for a more practical and rational approach to solving problems in society without involving supernatural beings.

Moreover, the Chinese school of Legalism, which became dominant during the Qin dynasty (221-206 BCE), also de-emphasized the role of supernatural beings and preferred adherence to strict laws and regulations over religious or spiritual piety.

2.1.4 Summary

So, as we can see, atheism and non-belief are not merely modern phenomena. The ancient world was brimming with skepticism, critical thinking, and alternative explanations for the universe's existence without relying on divine intervention or supernatural entities. These ancient roots of atheism laid the foundation for modern atheistic thought, which has evolved and adapted to the ever-changing world.

Hellenistic Philosophy and the Emergence of Skepticism

The history of atheism is often traced back to classical antiquity, an era marked by rapid social and political transformations, as well as burgeoning intellectual pursuits. It was a time that saw a shift in focus from traditional pantheons of gods and goddesses to one that revolved around the capacity of human reasoning and empirical inquiry.

One notable branch of ancient thought that bears considerable relevance on this subject is the Hellenistic philosophies. Sprouting from the 4th century BCE and onward, these schools of thought emerged as successors to the illustrious Classical Greek intellectual traditions nurtured by Socrates, Plato, and Aristotle. The shift from city-states to empires during the reign of Alexander the Great and the subsequent Hellenistic period prompted a new wave of intellectual inquiry that laid the foundation for future ideologies such as atheism.

The three main Hellenistic schools of thought that contributed to atheistic thought were Epicureanism, Stoicism, and Skepticism. Each possessed varying degrees of criticism and skepticism about religious beliefs.

Epicureanism

Epicureanism, named after its founder Epicurus (341-270 BCE), held a materialistic worldview that posited the existence of only atoms and the void. In Epicurus' view, gods existed but were completely detached from the mortal realm, and did not interfere with human affairs. Furthermore, they did not create the universe – rather, it came into being through a random series of atomic interactions.

Epicureanism countered the idea of divine retribution, denying that natural phenomena like earthquakes and storms were manifestations of divine wrath. Instead, they were purely material events with material causes. This perspective sharply deviated from traditional religious beliefs where gods were responsible for both natural occurrences and human welfare.

Although Epicureanism did not altogether discard the existence of gods, it certainly challenged conventional religious precepts and led to the emergence of deism, which held that God created the world but remained indifferent to its affairs thereafter.

Stoicism

Stoicism, founded by Zeno of Citium (circa 334-262 BCE), propounded the existence of divine elements within all beings, and that a rational and ethical life would bring about harmony with the 'cosmic reason', also known as the 'logos'. Though this philosophy was theistic in its orientations, the conception of the divine differed tremendously from established religious doctrines.

Unlike traditional religions that advocated for devotion to various gods and goddesses, Stoicism interpreted the divine as an inseparable part of human reasoning. This core stoic idea prompted followers to adopt principles of rationality, mindfulness, and self-control over supplication to deities.

Skepticism

Arguably the Hellenistic school of thought that is the most influential on atheism is Skepticism. It is most exemplified in the works of Pyrrho of Elis (circa 360-270 BCE) and Sextus Empiricus (circa 160-210 CE). The Skeptical approach emphasized the necessity of suspending judgement, given the contradictory nature of perceptions, beliefs, and arguments. Skeptics refrained from committing to any single metaphysical, ethical, or theological claim in order to avoid dogmatism.

The Skeptic's stance was most pertinently exhibited in their approach to religious matters, where they engaged in a systematic critique of popular religious beliefs. Sextus Empiricus' extensive critical examination of theistic arguments played a noteworthy role in shaping subsequent atheistic thought.

The Legacy of Hellenistic Philosophy

These influential schools of Hellenistic thought provided a common thread of questioning the veracity of religious claims and encouraging rational and critical inquiry into matters of belief. Though not entirely atheistic in and of themselves, they served as a springboard for the development of atheist thought in subsequent intellectual eras. The Hellenistic period witnessed the inception of a human-centric view of life, one that would eventually evolve into a thoroughly atheistic worldview in modern times.

3. Exploring Atheist Philosophies: From Materialism to Humanism

3.1 Materialism: The Foundation of Atheist Philosophies

Materialism is a philosophical view that asserts that all that exists is matter or physical substance, and anything non-material, such as gods, spirits or souls, is considered non-existent or illusory. This core belief is also sometimes referred to as physicalism or naturalism. Materialism is an important foundation for many atheist philosophies as it emphasizes the importance of understanding the natural world through empirical observation, reason and science, while providing a framework to dismiss supernatural claims that rely on faith or belief.

3.1.1 Historical Development of Materialism

The roots of materialism can be traced back to ancient civilizations, with various philosophers throughout history providing insights and theories that have built upon this basic worldview. Some key figures in the development of materialism include:

- **Thales of Miletus (c. 624–546 BCE)**: An ancient Greek philosopher, often known as the "father of materialism," Thales theorized that water was the common substance from which all things were made, placing focus on the material world as the basis for understanding reality.
- **Democritus (c. 460–370 BCE)**: Another ancient Greek philosopher who expanded upon the ideas of Thales, Democritus is best known for his theory of atomism. He postulated that everything in the universe is made of small, indivisible, and indestructible atoms moving in empty space.

- **Thomas Hobbes (1588–1679)**: An English philosopher known for his work in political philosophy, Hobbes argued that all phenomena, including human thoughts and emotions, could be explained in terms of matter in motion. He viewed the universe as a materialistic machine, governed by the laws of nature.
- **Baron d'Holbach (1723–1789)**: A French-German philosopher and encyclopedist, d'Holbach was a key figure in the Age of Enlightenment and one of the first outspoken atheists in Europe. He was a strong advocate for materialism, dismissing the existence of anything beyond the material world.
- **Friedrich Engels (1820–1895)**: A German philosopher and social scientist, Engels is well-known for his collaboration with Karl Marx. He developed the concept of dialectical materialism, which combined materialism with Hegelian dialectics to provide a framework for understanding the development of human history and society.

3.1.2 Key Concepts and Terminology

- **Determinism**: Materialism often goes hand in hand with determinism, the belief that all events and actions are determined by the interplay of material causes and effects. Determinism undermines the notions of free will and personal responsibility, as everything is ultimately the result of physical processes.
- **Reductionism**: Materialism can be seen as reductionist in nature, as it asserts that complex phenomena, including human emotions and consciousness, can be reduced to simpler, physical processes. This can be contrasted with other worldviews that acknowledge more complex or abstract, non-material components to reality.

- **Empiricism**: Materialism places a strong emphasis on empirical observation, reason and the scientific method as the primary means of understanding the world. By focusing on what can be observed and tested, materialism provides a foundation for the rejection of supernatural claims and beliefs that depend solely on faith.

3.1.3 Materialism and Atheism

While materialism does not necessarily entail atheism, the two positions are closely related, as they both reject the existence of non-material entities such as gods, spirits or souls. Atheists often find themselves drawn to materialistic theories as they provide a naturalistic explanation of the world that eschews supernatural claims. Materialism also forms a basis for secular ethics and humanism, which will be explored further in the following subsections.

3.2 Humanism: A Positive, Ethical Alternative to Religious Worldviews

Humanism is a broad philosophical perspective that focuses on the potential and agency of human beings, emphasizing reason, ethics, and empathy. While humanism often overlaps with atheism, it is not merely a rejection of religious beliefs; it is a positive, ethical stance that provides an alternative to traditional religious worldviews. Many atheists embrace humanist principles, and the term "secular humanism" is often used to connect these ideas with a specifically non-religious perspective.

3.2.1 Characteristics of Humanism

While humanism encompasses a diverse array of perspectives and ideas, there are several key characteristics that are often associated with humanist thought:

- **Rationality and empiricism**: Humanists place a strong emphasis on reason, critical thinking, and the scientific method as the best ways to understand the world and make sound decisions. This is in contrast to relying on faith, tradition, or religious authority.
- **Ethics**: Humanists affirm the importance of ethical principles and values that are based on human needs and interests, rather than divine commandments. Humanist ethics are often grounded in empathy, cooperation, and the promotion of human flourishing.
- **Individual dignity and autonomy**: Humanism emphasizes the unique worth and dignity of each individual, advocating for personal autonomy and the freedom to make one's own choices in life.
- **Democracy and social justice**: Humanists often support democratic institutions, the rule of law, and the promotion of social justice, striving for a more equitable society that ensures the well-being and fulfillment of all people.
- **Naturalism**: Many humanists adopt a naturalistic worldview, which assumes that everything that exists is part of the natural world and rejects supernatural claims.

3.2.2 The Evolution of Humanism

Humanism has deep historical roots that can be traced back to various intellectual and cultural movements throughout history, including:

- **Ancient Greece and Rome**: Humanism draws inspiration from the works of ancient philosophers,

such as Socrates, Plato, and Aristotle, who emphasized reason, the search for truth, and the importance of ethical living.
- **The Renaissance**: During the Renaissance, humanism emerged as a cultural movement that championed the study of the classical texts, arts, and values of ancient Greece and Rome, and fostered the development of the humanities as intellectual disciplines.
- **The Enlightenment**: The Enlightenment saw the burgeoning of humanist thought, with philosophers such as Immanuel Kant, David Hume, and John Locke advocating for reason, skepticism, and the importance of individual rights.
- **Modern Secular Humanism**: In the 19th and 20th centuries, humanism evolved into an explicitly non-religious perspective that incorporated elements of materialism, atheism, and secularism. Key figures in the development of modern secular humanism include Robert Ingersoll, Bertrand Russell, and John Dewey.

3.2.3 Humanism and Atheism

Humanism offers a positive ethical framework that many atheists find appealing, as it provides values and principles that are grounded in human experience, rather than religious beliefs. By embracing humanism, atheists are able to affirm their moral convictions and strive for a more compassionate, rational, and just world without relying on supernatural claims or divine authority.

3.1 Materialism and Naturalism: The World as It Is

Before we dive into the various philosophies associated with atheism, it is crucial to understand the fundamental assumption underlying most atheist thought – materialism. Materialism (also known as physicalism) is the belief that everything in the universe is made up of matter and that everything can be explained in terms of material interactions.

3.1.1 Materialism: The Foundations of Atheism

The materialist philosophy is closely related to the scientific method, which seeks to understand the universe in terms of observable, measurable, and testable phenomena. This perspective stands in stark contrast to religious and supernatural explanations, which often invoke deities, divine intervention, or supernatural powers to explain the world.

Materialism is attractive to atheists because it offers a clear and concise framework for understanding the world without the need for religious belief. It demands evidence for any claim made about the nature of reality and dismisses unproven or untestable assertions. This skepticism leads to a rejection of religious notions about gods, souls, and afterlives.

3.1.2 Naturalism: A Refined Materialism

A more refined version of materialism is known as naturalism. Naturalism extends the materialist commitment to the view that everything in the universe can be understood through natural processes and laws rather than supernatural or divine intervention.

Naturalism goes beyond materialism by emphasizing the importance of empirical evidence, observation, and testing. This viewpoint aligns well with modern scientific methods and has been highly successful in explaining various phenomena – ranging from the vast expanses of the universe to the smallest particles within atoms.

Both materialism and naturalism share a common feature – the denial of anything supernatural or divine, which often leads their adherents to embrace atheism as a logical extension of their worldviews.

3.2 Existentialism: The Search for Meaning in a Godless World

One of the most prominent and influential philosophical movements within atheism is existentialism. While some existentialist philosophers did hold religious or theistic beliefs, many others adopted atheistic perspectives because of the movement's emphasis on human existence, individual freedom, and responsibility.

3.2.1 Existentialism: A Focus on the Human Condition

At its core, existentialism is concerned with the individual's experience of existence, the subjective nature of reality, and the process of finding meaning and purpose in life. Existentialist philosophers delve into questions about the nature of human existence, the human condition, and the limits and possibilities of human knowledge.

For many atheistic existentialists, the absence of God means that individuals must create their own meaning and purpose in life. This notion is often condensed into the saying, "existence precedes essence." In other words, human beings are born without an inherent purpose or identity, but through their experiences and actions, they must define themselves and create a meaningful existence.

3.2.2 The Existentialists: Major Thinkers and Ideas

Key atheistic existentialist philosophers include Jean-Paul Sartre, Albert Camus, and Friedrich Nietzsche. These thinkers, among others, emphasized the importance of free will, authenticity, and responsibility in shaping one's life.

Sartre, for example, famously asserted, "Man is condemned to be free; because once thrown into the world, he is responsible for everything he does." This idea highlights the significance of personal choice and the weight of responsibility in creating a meaningful life.

Camus, on the other hand, initiated the concept of "the absurd" – the idea that the search for meaning in an indifferent and irrational universe is inherently futile. However, Camus argued that recognizing and embracing this absurdity allows one to live an authentic and meaningful life.

3.3 Humanism: Building a Better World Through Reason and Compassion

Another significant atheist philosophy is humanism, which centers on reason, ethics, and compassion as essential components of human life. Humanism rejects the notion of divine or supernatural influences in favor of a focus on human beings as the agents of change and progress.

3.3.1 Humanism: A Life Guided by Reason and Empathy

Humanism emphasizes the critical role of reason, science, and intellect in understanding the world and shaping human life. It rejects religious dogma, superstition, and blind faith in favor of critical thinking and the pursuit of truth.

In addition to advocating for a rational and evidence-based approach to life, humanism also champions compassion, empathy, and social justice. Humanism encourages individuals to look beyond themselves and consider the welfare of others and their community. It promotes moral and ethical behaviors founded on principles of human dignity, respect, and justice.

3.3.2 Secular Humanism: Humanism Without God

While some humanist philosophies incorporate religious or spiritual elements, secular humanism is explicitly atheistic. Secular humanists argue that a moral and purposeful life can be achieved without belief in a god or afterlife. Instead, they focus on human beings' capacity for empathy, reason, and ethical behavior.

Secular humanism celebrates human achievements in science, reason, and cultural development, asserting that these accomplishments demonstrate our capacity to build a better world grounded in human values.

Secular humanism has influenced many modern atheistic thinkers and activists, including Richard Dawkins, Sam Harris, and Daniel Dennett, who have advocated for atheism, reason, and evidence-based ethics in their writings and public appearances.

3.4 In Conclusion: A Spectrum of Atheist Philosophies

Despite sharing a disbelief in gods or supernatural forces, atheist philosophies are diverse and varied. Materialism, existentialism, and humanism are just a few examples of philosophies with wide-ranging implications for the study of human knowledge, morality, and purpose.

The exploration of these different perspectives showcases the richness and depth of atheism as a philosophical tradition, far from being a mere negation of religious beliefs. Believers and non-believers alike can appreciate the insights and inspiration found in these worldviews, as they grapple with some of the most profound questions about the human existence.

3.1 Materialism: Understanding the Physical Basis of Reality

3.1.1 Defining Materialism

Materialism is a philosophical standpoint that asserts that all things can be explained in terms of matter, energy, and their interactions. It posits that everything that exists—from the smallest particles to the largest galaxies and everything in between, including our thoughts, emotions, and actions— can be reduced to physical phenomena.

In materialism, there is no need to postulate the existence of God, spirits, or other supernatural entities, as everything is ultimately the product of natural laws and the interactions of physical constituents. Hence, materialism provides a naturalistic and parsimonious framework for understanding the world and has served as a foundational perspective for many atheists.

3.1.2 Materialism in Science and Philosophy

The materialist worldview has had a significant influence on the development of scientific thought. Pioneering scientists of the Scientific Revolution, such as Galileo Galilei and Sir Isaac Newton, were heavily influenced by material ideas as they sought to explain the natural world using empirical evidence and mathematical descriptions.

Over time, advancements in scientific knowledge have only provided more support for the materialist perspective. For instance, the groundbreaking work of Charles Darwin established the theory of evolution, which demonstrates how complex life forms, including humans, can emerge from purely material processes. Physics, too, provides powerful support for materialism, detailing the fundamental forces, particles, and interactions that govern the universe.

Beyond its scientific implications, materialism also permeates much of Western philosophy. The ancient Greek philosopher Democritus, for example, first proposed the idea of atoms, the indivisible and indestructible building blocks of reality, which laid the groundwork for materialism as a worldview.

3.1.3 Critiques of Materialism

Despite its many achievements, materialism is not without its limitations and criticisms. Several important philosophical questions remain unanswered within the materialist framework. Some of these questions include the nature of consciousness, free will, and morality.

Dualists and immaterialists argue that materialism is insufficient to explain the subjective nature of human consciousness. They believe that mental phenomena like thoughts, emotions, and consciousness itself cannot be fully explained by a purely physical account of the brain and its processes. Some philosophers, like David Chalmers, argue that the "hard problem" of consciousness — how subjective experience arises from objective neural activity — may never be resolved within the materialist paradigm.

Moreover, the issue of free will is a complex area of debate within philosophical materialism. Some materialists argue that human actions are fully determined by the laws of physics, much like the motion of a complex machine. This deterministic view ultimately dismisses the notion of human agency, accountability, and personal responsibility. Other materialists acknowledge that free will remains a significant challenge to their worldview, and work to develop alternative notions of agency compatible with a physicalist description of reality.

3.1.4 Materialism and Atheism

For many atheists, materialism provides a compelling and consistent framework for understanding the world without reference to supernatural beliefs. It grounds the atheist worldview in empirical evidence and scientific inquiry, offering a naturalistic account of reality that stands in contrast to theistic claims about the existence of a supernatural creator or divine beings.

However, it is important to recognize that atheism and materialism are not synonymous. One can be an atheist without being a strict materialist, and some atheists maintain various forms of non-materialist philosophies. Nonetheless, materialism remains a popular and influential position for many atheists and provides a firm foundation in science and reason from which to explore alternative perspectives on existence and meaning.

3.2 Humanism: Focusing on Human Values and Well-being

3.2.1 Defining Humanism

Humanism is a philosophical perspective that emphasizes human welfare, progress, and the innate worth of individuals. Humanism is focused on promoting the happiness and well-being of all people, without reliance on divine intervention or support from supernatural entities. Humanism shares many core values with atheism, such as reason, critical thinking, and skepticism, while emphasizing the importance of compassion, morality, and social justice.

Humanism can be broadly traced back to the works of ancient Greek philosophers, who stressed the central role of human reason and rationality in making sense of the world, and to the Enlightenment, which saw human flourishing and progress as the ultimate aims of society. Today, humanism is a common philosophy for atheists who seek to cultivate ethical lives in the absence of religious beliefs.

3.2.2 Secular Ethics and Morality

One of the primary concerns of humanist philosophy is constructing a secular system of ethics that does not rely on divine authority or supernatural principles. Humanism posits that human beings are capable of developing moral frameworks based on reason, empathy, and shared values. Many humanists subscribe to consequentialist ethics, which focuses on the results of actions, or to virtue ethics, which emphasizes the cultivation of character and the development of ethical virtues.

Humanism also stresses the importance of secular institutions and society in promoting ethical behavior and moral development. Institutions like education, justice, and governance all have a role to play in shaping the moral character of individuals and fostering responsible and compassionate citizens.

3.2.3 Humanism and Life's Purpose

Humanism offers a powerful response to the question of life's purpose and meaning in a world without religious beliefs. Humanists argue that, in the absence of an externally conferred purpose or supernatural plan, individuals are free to create their own meaning and purpose by shaping their lives around personal values, relationships, and experiences.

Humanists recognize that while the universe may not have a transcendent purpose, human life is still inherently valuable, and individuals have an almost limitless capacity to positively shape the world around them, improving the lives of others and leaving a lasting impact on society. Thus, the humanist approach to life's meaning is both empowering and deeply fulfilling, grounded in compassion and the shared pursuit of progress and well-being.

3.2.4 Humanism and Atheism

Humanism serves as an ethical and philosophical grounding for many atheists, providing a positive and life-affirming worldview that transcends a mere rejection of religious belief. By focusing on human values, progress, and well-being, humanism demonstrates that atheists can lead lives of purpose, beauty, and moral integrity without resorting to supernatural justifications or divine guidance.

However, it is important to note that humanism and atheism are not interchangeable terms. Not all atheists are humanists, and conceivably, one could be a humanist without being an atheist. Nonetheless, humanism offers a rich philosophical tradition that echoes many of the core commitments of atheism and provides a compelling alternative to theistic worldviews.

In conclusion, materialism and humanism represent just two of the diverse array of philosophies supporting the atheist worldview. Materialism provides a naturalistic and scientifically grounded approach to reality, whereas humanism emphasizes human values and ethical considerations without relying on supernatural explanations. Both of these philosophies contribute to a broader understanding of the world, allowing atheists to engage in meaningful lives characterized by truth-seeking, moral integrity, and commitment to the well-being of all.

4. The Logic of Atheism: Debunking Theistic Arguments

4.1 The Cosmological Argument and Its Inadequacies

The Cosmological Argument is one of the most famous and widely discussed theistic arguments. At its core, it tries to establish a causal relationship between the existence of the universe and the need for a "cause" – in other words, a deity. To explore this argument and the various ways in which atheists have debunked it, let us first examine some of the most influential versions of the argument.

4.1.1 The Kalam Cosmological Argument

The Kalam Cosmological Argument can be summed up as follows:

1. Everything that begins to exist has a cause.
2. The universe began to exist
3. Therefore, the universe has a cause.

In this syllogism, the key premise is the second one: the contention that the universe began to exist. Atheists have successfully punctured this claim in multiple ways. For one thing, invoking a deity is not the only way to explain the origin of the universe. The field of cosmology has offered several natural, non-theistic explanations, such as the Big Bang Theory or the theory of the multiverse. Moreover, the introduction of a supernatural being would hardly resolve the problem of infinite regression: if everything that begins to exist has a cause, who or what created the deity?

4.1.2 The Leibnizian Cosmological Argument

Gottfried Wilhelm Leibniz, a German philosopher and mathematician, developed his Cosmological Argument along these lines:

1. Everything that exists has an explanation, either in the necessity of its own nature or in an external cause.
2. If the universe has an explanation, that explanation is God.
3. The universe exists.
4. Therefore, the universe has an explanation (from 1 and 3).
5. Therefore, the explanation of the universe is God (from 2 and 4).

At first glance, this argument might appear more convincing than the Kalam version, as it relies less on the temporal aspect of the universe's beginning. Nevertheless, its second premise is highly debatable: why should we assume that the explanation for the universe's existence must be a deity? Atheists might argue that scientific theories, like those mentioned above, can supply that explanation without recourse to a supernatural being.

Additionally, the first premise might be approached from a different angle. Everything that we have observed and experienced has taken place within our own universe; that is, within the singular context of space and time. Thus, it may be unwarranted – or even meaningless – to apply the principles of causality, explanation, and necessity to the universe as a whole. This challenges the very foundation of the argument.

4.1.3 The Thomistic Cosmological Argument

Thomas Aquinas, the medieval philosopher, and theologian, posited another widely-recognized rendition of the Cosmological Argument. In the "Five Ways" section of his work *Summa Theologica*, he intended to provide proofs of God's existence, one of which can be paraphrased as follows:

1. Some things in the universe are in motion.
2. Anything that is in motion must be set in motion by something else.
3. If we trace back the chain of movers, there must be a First Mover that set everything else in motion.
4. The First Mover is God.

Atheists have objected to this argument on several grounds. Once again, the issue of infinite regression arises: if everything must be set in motion by something else, what caused God's very first act of motion? Furthermore, why should we assume that the First Mover has the characteristics typically assigned to a deity (such as omnipotence, omniscience, and benevolence)? The concept of a "First Mover" could be applied to a natural, non-theistic phenomenon, such as the Big Bang. Lastly, modern physics has complicated the ancient theoretical frameworks of motion and causality: quantum mechanics, for instance, allows for events to occur without a clear, determinable cause.

4.1.4 Conclusion

When scrutinized, the Cosmological Argument and its various iterations fail to provide a convincing proof for the existence of a deity. Atheists can respond to each version with counterarguments rooted in science, logic, and epistemology. By undermining the foundations of these theistic claims, atheism demonstrates its logical coherence and intellectual viability.

4.1 The Cosmological Argument: Challenging the Need for a First Cause

Cosmological arguments aim to demonstrate that there must be a necessary, uncaused first cause of the universe. They generally take the form of trying to demonstrate that an infinite regress of causes is impossible, and therefore, a first cause must exist. While this argument has numerous variations, we will focus on the Kalam Cosmological Argument as representative of the general approach. The argument posits:

1. Everything that begins to exist has a cause.
2. The universe began to exist.
3. Therefore, the universe has a cause.

4.1.1 Critiquing Premise One: The Arbitrary Limit

The first premise, that everything that begins to exist has a cause, may at first seem reasonable. However, the phrase "begins to exist" is arbitrary, serving to limit the premise to the kinds of things a theist feels they can comfortably attribute to their deity (e.g., the universe). Arguably, anything that 'begins to exist' is merely rearranged matter and energy. The wood from a tree begins to exist as a chair, but does this mean a supernatural cause must be invoked? Clearly not, and yet the premise seems to apply better to chairs than to gods or universes.

Furthermore, the premise contradicts itself if applied to the deity in question. If everything that begins to exist has a cause, then the deity itself would also need a cause. The theist may argue their deity did not "begin to exist", but this shifts the focus onto defining what is meant by "beginning to exist". As we currently lack any coherent or useful definitions that exempt the deity, the first premise is rendered arbitrary and incoherent.

4.1.2 Critiquing Premise Two: Facing Our Ignorance About the Universe

The second premise is an assertion that the universe began to exist. This assumes both that the concept of "beginning to exist" makes sense when applied to the universe and that it is indeed true that the universe has a beginning. The former point has already been questioned, while the latter is a matter of open debate among cosmologists, physicists, and philosophers.

While the predominant view influenced by the Big Bang Theory suggests a 'beginning' to our universe, there are alternative theories/models that do not posit such a distinct origin point. For example, it is plausible that our universe is part of a larger multiverse or that it may undergo cyclic periods of contraction and expansion. Until conclusive evidence settles these questions, using the "beginning" of the universe as a premise is far from convincing.

4.1.3 The Unsupported Conclusion: From First Cause to Deity

Even if the cosmological argument were sound, it only establishes that the universe has a cause. Drawing the conclusion that this cause is a particular deity, or any deity at all, requires an additional argument. Many properties typically attributed to gods (e.g., omniscience, omnipotence, benevolence) do not necessarily follow from the concept of a first cause.

At best, the argument might support deism, the belief in a non-interventionist creator that does not engage in further miracles, revelation, or interaction with humanity as understood by theistic systems such as Christianity, Islam, or Hinduism. However, even deistic conclusions arguably go too far when positing the nature of a first cause.

4.2 The Teleological Argument: Questioning Design and Purpose

Teleological arguments, often referred to as arguments from design, claim that the complexity and orderliness of nature or the universe indicate the existence of an intelligent designer. Among these arguments are the Fine-Tuning Argument, Intelligent Design, and the Argument from Biological Complexity. In response to these assertions, atheists can propose various counterarguments.

4.2.1 Mistaking Apparent Design for Actual Design

At first glance, the complexity and order found in nature might seem like evidence of an intelligent designer. However, evolutionary processes such as natural selection and genetic drift demonstrate how complex and ordered systems can emerge without a conscious guide. Features or functions that appear to be designed result from the gradual refinement of random mutations through competition and environmental pressures.

For example, the human eye might appear to be an instance of deliberate design, but the gradual evolution of light-sensitive spots into sophisticated optical instruments over millions of years of evolutionary history offers a compelling alternative explanation.

4.2.2 Evaluating the Arguments from Fine-Tuning and Intelligent Design

4.2 Common Theistic Arguments and Their Rebuttals

In this section, we examine the common theistic claims and their respective rebuttals. One of the purposes of this section is not only to provide cogent counterarguments but also to highlight the importance of critical thinking and reasoning when discussing the existence of God.

4.2.1 The Cosmological Argument

The Cosmological Argument contends that the universe must have a cause or explanation for its existence, which is typically identified as God. The most well-known versions of this argument are the Kalam Cosmological Argument and the Leibnizian Cosmological Argument.

Kalam Cosmological Argument:

1. Everything that begins to exist has a cause.
2. The universe began to exist.
3. Therefore, the universe has a cause.

Leibnizian Cosmological Argument:

1. Everything that exists has an explanation of its existence, either in the necessity of its own nature or in an external cause.
2. The universe exists.
3. Therefore, the universe has an explanation of its existence in an external cause.

Rebuttal:

One common rebuttal to these arguments is concerned with the nature and origin of God. If God exists as the eternal, uncaused cause of the universe, then it seems we can ask why God exists, rather than the universe itself being eternal or uncaused. Moreover, if one posits that God needs no explanation for its existence, then why can we not make the same claim for the universe? This would invalidate the core assumption of these arguments, making the specific postulation of God unnecessary and insufficient.

Another major objection is the application of causality to the universe as a whole. Causality, as we understand it, operates within the confines of space and time. However, the universe contains both space and time, raising questions about whether our current comprehension of causality can truly be extrapolated to explain the entire universe. This objection exposes our limited human understanding of causality and how it may be inapplicable or require reevaluation when discussing the origin of the universe itself.

4.2.2 The Teleological Argument

The Teleological Argument, or Argument from Design, proposes that the intricate and complex organization found in the universe and living beings must be the result of deliberate design by an intelligent designer, which is traditionally identified as God. The most famous example of this argument is the watchmaker analogy, which compares the precise and ordered nature of the universe to an expertly crafted watch, implying that both require a conscious creator.

Rebuttal:

The most comprehensive rebuttal to the Teleological Argument is provided by Charles Darwin's theory of evolution by natural selection. This scientific theory demonstrates that the complexity and organization of living organisms are a result of a natural, unguided process that produces adaptive traits advantageous for survival and reproduction, rather than the result of intentional design. This explanation eliminates the need for an intelligent designer to account for biological complexity.

Additionally, the Teleological Argument commits the fallacy of false analogy. Comparing the universe or living organisms to a watch ignores the vast differences between them, and subsequently assumes that because one has a designer, all must have a designer. This fallacy is further exposed when considering suboptimal features in nature such as vestigial organs or the human appendix, which undermine the argument for a perfect or intelligent designer.

4.2.3 The Moral Argument

The Moral Argument posits that the existence of objective moral values and duties implies the existence of a moral lawgiver, which is identified as God. Without this lawgiver, all moral values and duties would be subjective or nonexistent.

Rebuttal:

One notable rebuttal to this argument comes from ethical theories such as utilitarianism or Kantian ethics, which provide secular explanations for objective moral values and duties without the necessity of a supernatural creator.

Additionally, the Euthyphro Dilemma, originally posed by Plato, highlights potential flaws in the Moral Argument. This dilemma asks whether an action is moral because God commands it or God commands it because it is moral. If the former is true, then morality is arbitrary, depending solely on what God commands, which makes it subjective. If the latter is true, then morality exists independently of God, indicating that objective moral values and duties can exist without a moral lawgiver.

4.2.4 Ontological Argument

The Ontological Argument is an a priori argument, which means it does not rely on empirical evidence, but rather on pure reasoning. It posits that the concept of a perfect being necessarily entails its existence, as existing is greater or more perfect than not existing.

Rebuttal:

One major objection against the Ontological Argument comes from philosopher Immanuel Kant, who asserts that existence is not a property or predicate that changes the essence or nature of a being. For instance, a non-existent unicorn or an existent unicorn both have the same definition of a unicorn. Stating that something exists or not does not change its properties or definition. Therefore, the concept of existence does not contribute to a being's essence or perfection, and so the argument fails.

In conclusion, it is essential to approach arguments for the existence of God with an open and critical mindset, carefully examining assumptions, logic, and evidence. By doing so, we can explore the limitations and flaws in these theistic arguments to construct a robust, rational foundation for atheism.

5. Morality Without God: Establishing Secular Ethics

5.1 Foundations of Secular Ethics

One of the most common objections raised against atheism is the perceived loss (or lack) of a reliable moral compass. Many theists argue that without belief in a higher power, there can be no objective basis for morality, and that secular ethics are merely arbitrary and non-binding. However, proponents of secular ethics argue that a moral framework can be developed without any reliance on divine commandments or supernatural forces.

5.1.1 Values and Principles

Secular ethics typically begins with the acknowledgement that humans are social animals who have evolved to live in cooperative groups with shared values and principles. These values can be seen as the basic building blocks of any moral framework, regardless of whether or not one believes in God. They include:

- Respect for human life
- Fairness and justice
- Compassion and empathy
- Honesty and truth-telling
- Personal integrity and responsibility
- Respect for the autonomy of others

These values are not unique to any particular religion or cultural tradition, but instead represent a shared human heritage. As social animals, our survival and flourishing depend on our ability to work together in organized communities with shared norms and standards. Thus, we develop morality as a natural outcome of our social nature.

5.1.2 Reason and Empathy as Moral Guides

Secular ethics relies on reason, empathy, and the consideration of the well-being of others as the primary guides for determining right and wrong. Using these guides, we can derive objective moral principles that are independent of any religious teachings or divine commands.

By examining the effects of our actions on the well-being of others, we can use reason to evaluate the consequences of our actions and make moral choices based on a rational assessment of those consequences. Furthermore, empathy allows us to connect with and understand the experiences of others, helping us to consider their needs and promote their well-being alongside our own.

5.1.3 The Golden Rule and Reciprocity

Reciprocity is a key concept in secular ethics, echoing the age-old idea of the Golden Rule: "Treat others as you would like to be treated." This principle serves as a basic guideline for making moral decisions and fosters cooperation among individuals within a community. By promoting reciprocal behavior, we encourage a more harmonious and empathic society.

The Golden Rule represents a simple, yet powerful, moral principle that transcends religious and cultural boundaries, making it an ideal foundation for secular ethics. Moreover, it aligns with our natural tendencies for empathy and cooperation and can be rationally justified by appealing to our shared interests in mutual well-being.

5.1.4 Utilitarianism and the Greatest Happiness Principle

Utilitarianism provides another approach to secular ethics, focusing on the maximization of well-being or happiness. Often summarized as "the greatest happiness for the greatest number," utilitarianism encourages actions that will bring about the best overall consequences for all those affected by our decisions.

This consequentialist philosophy relies on reason and compassion to guide moral decision-making, as individuals must carefully assess the likely outcomes of their actions to determine what will bring about the greatest benefit for everyone involved. Although utilitarianism sometimes faces criticism for potentially sacrificing individual rights in the pursuit of overall happiness, it remains an important and influential framework within secular ethics.

5.1.5 Humanism, Dignity, and Rights

Humanism is a philosophical and ethical stance that emphasizes the value and agency of human beings, individually and collectively. Rooted in the belief that human beings have the ability to create meaning and shape their own destinies, humanism places great importance on the promotion of human dignity, rights, and social justice.

Secular ethics can also draw upon the concept of human rights as a means of promoting fairness, equality, and universal moral principles. By recognizing that all humans should have basic rights and protections, regardless of their religion, ethnicity, or cultural background, we can build a solid foundation for secular ethics based on common humanity rather than divine authority.

###- In conclusion

Secular ethics offers a robust and rational alternative to religious-based moral frameworks, drawing upon shared human values, reason, empathy, reciprocal behavior, and the promotion of well-being. This approach fosters a more inclusive, compassionate, and democratic form of morality, capable of addressing contemporary ethical challenges and creating a fair and just society for all.

5.2: The Importance of Secular Ethics

Overview

The question of how to establish a solid ethical framework in the absence of divine guidance has long been a central issue for atheists and religious critics. This section will take a closer look at how secular ethics can provide a viable and even superior alternative for crafting a moral code.

The Problems with Divine Command Theory

Divine command theory, the idea that moral principles stem directly from the will of God, has been a prominent justification for ethical rules in religious contexts, but it suffers from several issues:

1. **Reliance on an unproven premise**: The fundamental premise of divine command theory is that moral authority comes from God. However, the existence of a deity is a belief many atheists do not share, making this foundation unreliable for building a secular ethical system.
2. **Arbitrary nature of commands**: Even if we were to assume the existence of God, divine command theory leaves us with a disturbing conclusion that morality is contingent on God's whims, making it intrinsically arbitrary, and therefore, morally suspect. This is the well-known Euthyphro dilemma: if actions are moral only because God commands them, is there really an

underlying moral reason, or are we simply following moral conventions for the sake of obedience?

3. **Interpretive and cultural issues**: There are vast disagreements between and within religious traditions on various moral matters, like war, birth control, and treatment of animals. Given these conflicting interpretations, it's unclear how to derive a universally applicable moral code that would satisfy all believers.

The Basis of Secular Ethics: Reason, Empathy, and Well-Being

Secularists argue that some of the most important foundations of ethical behavior can be found in innate human faculties like reason, empathy, and experiential knowledge. This makes secular ethics a natural project rooted in empirical, rational inquiry.

1. **Reason**: Our capacity for reasoning allows us to identify general principles that can help us navigate the complexities of existence. By carefully considering the potential consequences of our actions, discerning patterns over time, and using critical thinking to evaluate the validity of differing perspectives, we can construct ethical frameworks that prioritize what's logically best for our well-being.
2. **Empathy**: Our ability to empathize with others' feelings leads us to recognize their intrinsic value as sentient beings who experience happiness and suffering. Empathy can lead us to care about others' well-being, motivating us to act altruistically and find ways to mitigate harm.
3. **Well-Being**: Secular ethics often revolves around the goal of maximizing well-being for ourselves and others. This means recognizing the factors that can

contribute to a flourishing life, such as mental and physical health, social connections, fulfillment of basic needs, intellectual and creative pursuits, and fairness in our institutions.

Popular Secular Ethical Theories

Given these foundations, let's explore some secular ethical theories that have emerged as alternatives to reliance on divine commands.

1. **Utilitarianism**: This consequentialist theory, formulated by Jeremy Bentham and John Stuart Mill, posits that moral actions are those that maximize overall happiness and minimize suffering. In other words, the best decision is the one that brings the most net utility to all individuals involved.
2. **Deontology**: As proposed by Immanuel Kant, this moral framework emphasizes following moral rules or duties, rather than focusing on ends or consequences, and stresses treating other individuals as ends in themselves, never merely as tools. The most well-known principle within this system is the categorical imperative, which states that an action is only morally permissible if we can will it to become a universal law without contradicting ourselves.
3. **Virtue Ethics**: Going back to ancient Greek philosophers like Aristotle, this moral system focuses on the development of character traits as the basis for ethical life. By cultivating virtues such as honesty, courage, wisdom, and compassion, we become more attuned to making morally informed decisions and acting in accordance with our ethical values.
4. **Ethics of Care**: Drawing on feminist thought and insights from psychological research, the ethics of care emphasizes the importance of empathy,

attentiveness, and responsibility within relationships, rather than an externally imposed set of rules or principles.

Going Beyond the Basics

One of the key appeals of secular ethics is its adaptability, given its grounding in rational inquiry and empirical evidence. As social, cultural, and scientific circumstances change, our understanding of what it means to lead a moral life can evolve, allowing for the incorporation of diverse perspectives and emerging discoveries.

Some critical analytical tools that can enrich and expand secular ethics include:

1. **Intersectionality**: By recognizing the ways in which different types of identities, values, and experiences interact and intersect, we can develop a more nuanced understanding of ethical priorities and work towards solutions that are inclusive and sensitive to diverse needs.
2. **Environmentally-Informed Ethics**: Given the ecological challenges faced by today's world, integrating environmental considerations into secular moral thought can help guide actions that protect and sustain valuable natural resources, promote the well-being of all life on our planet, and ensure the health of future generations.
3. **Technologically-Informed Ethics**: As new technologies and innovations disrupt traditional ways of life, bring new risks, and raise new ethical questions, secular ethics is well-equipped to grapple with the implications for human society and values, taking into account both the potentials and pitfalls associated with technological advances.

Conclusion

Secular ethics, with its rational, empathetic, and evolving nature, can provide a robust and flexible ethical framework capable of guiding morally responsible choices that are better-suited to our diverse, ever-changing world. By drawing on our best cognitive and emotional capacities and constantly expanding our horizons with new ideas, secular ethics offers the promise of a better, more inclusive world.

5.1. The Euthyphro Dilemma: A Failed Divine Command Theory

Before discussing secular ethics, it is essential to address Divine Command Theory, a popular argument in the religious context that claims, moral values can only originate from a divine being, specifically God. According to this theory, an act is morally good if God commands it, whereas it is morally wrong if God forbids it. By refuting this claim, one can further establish the need for secular ethics.

The Euthyphro Dilemma, as recounted in Plato's dialogue Euthyphro, questions whether something is good because God commands it, or if God commands it because it is good. The ancient Greek philosopher, Socrates, explores this conundrum when discussing the nature of piety with Euthyphro. Their dialogue reveals two critical problems with tying morality solely to divine commands.

1. **If something is good because God commands it:** In this case, it implies that God's commands are arbitrary and could change at any time. God's choice to command actions like love, empathy, and honesty could have just as easily been commands to murder,

steal, or lie. This means that morality would be solely based on whims, making it fundamentally unstable and untrustworthy in establishing an ethical system.

2. **If God commands something because it is good:** In this scenario, it would imply that goodness exists independently of God, so the divine command is redundant. God recognizes the goodness in morality rather than being the source of it. Consequently, people can tap into that independent source of goodness and decide on their morals.

The Euthyphro Dilemma reveals the inherent flaws in the Divine Command Theory, making it an unsuitable foundation for establishing an ethical system. With that out of the way, let's embark on the journey of understanding secular ethics.

5.2. Humanism: The Cornerstone of Secular Morality

Humanism emphasizes human welfare, rationality, and critical thinking, rejecting any supernatural or divine intervention in determining morality. The focus shifts from supernatural beings to human beings and their experiences. At its core, humanism seeks the betterment of humanity and the natural world.

5.2.1. Utilitarianism: The Greatest Happiness Principle

Developed by philosophers such as Jeremy Bentham and John Stuart Mill, Utilitarianism is an ethical theory that emphasizes the maximization of overall happiness while minimizing suffering. This 'greatest happiness principle' is the foundation of Utilitarianism, which essentially means choosing the action that generates the most excellent overall well-being for all affected parties.

Utilitarianism is consequentialist, focusing on the results of actions rather than the inherent nature of the actions themselves. As a secular ethical framework, it offers a method for decision-making that relies on the measurable outcomes in terms of pleasure or pain.

5.2.2. Deontological Ethics: Duty and Rules

In contrast to Utilitarianism, Deontological Ethics (or duty-based ethics) revolves around adherence to rules or duties rather than consequences. German philosopher Immanuel Kant's philosophy heavily influences this ethical framework in his Categorical Imperative, which prescribes treating people as ends in themselves and never merely as a means to an end.

Kantian ethics provides a secular moral framework that does not rely on God or divine commandments. It encourages rationality, claiming that by exercising reason, humans can determine universally legislated moral duties that should be followed at all times, regardless of the consequences.

5.3. Empathy and Social Consequences: The Roots of Morality

At the heart of morality lie empathy and social consequences. As evolved social animals, humans possess the capacity to understand and share the feelings of others. This prosocial trait of empathy serves as an essential foundation for ethical behavior. Observable patterns of moral development in children show that empathy emerges early in life, even before they have been taught formal religious teachings or moral codes.

Beyond empathy, social consequences also play a role in shaping moral behavior. The need for a well-functioning society depends on its members cooperating with each other, presupposing some form of moral and ethical code. In-group loyalty, fairness, and justice are core moral values that have developed in societies through time – independent of religious scriptures or supernatural beings – to encourage social cohesion.

5.4. Conclusion: A Comprehensive, Secular Ethical Framework

In summary, establishing secular ethics is not only possible, but it is a crucial endeavor to ensure a rational and sustainable approach to morality. Rejecting an unstable and arbitrary Divine Command Theory, individuals can draw upon humanist philosophies, such as Utilitarianism and Deontological Ethics, to create a robust and secular ethical framework.

By recognizing the importance of empathy, social consequences, and human welfare, secular ethics transcends the need for divine or supernatural edicts, placing the onus on humanity to collectively determine and abide by a system of morality that contributes to the betterment of all.

The exploration of secular ethics equips atheists, agnostics, and non-believers alike with a rich foundation for moral decision-making and ethical living that is rationally grounded, compassionate, and intrinsically human.

6. Religion vs. Science: The Battle for Truth

6.1 The Historical Conflict between Religion and Science

The relationship between religion and science has undergone considerable evolution throughout human history. Science and religion, as systems of thought and belief, have helped humans understand and make sense of the world around them. While many believe that these two systems can coexist harmoniously, there have been numerous instances of conflict between them—especially concerning their interpretations of the cosmos and natural phenomena.

6.1.1 Early Encounters: From Ancient Times to the Middle Ages

The early encounters between religion and science can be traced back to ancient civilizations, such as Egypt, Mesopotamia, India, China, and Greece. During these times, scientific knowledge was limited and religious explanations of natural phenomena were prevalent. This is reflected in the cultures' mythologies, which often featured gods and supernatural beings responsible for the creation and maintenance of the universe.

In India, for example, the complex Vedic religion incorporated astronomical observations into its religious rituals, while Chinese cosmological beliefs were strongly influenced by their understanding of astronomy. Moreover, ancient Greeks, such as Pythagoras and Plato, integrated philosophical ideas and mathematical principles into their religious views. The fusion of scientific and religious thought continued into the Middle Ages, with Islamic scholars contributing to the development of both natural sciences and theology.

However, the coexistence of religion and science was not without tension. Some ancient thinkers, such as the pre-Socratic philosopher Democritus, proposed naturalistic explanations of the universe, devoid of spiritual or supernatural elements, which contrasted with the prevailing religious perspectives. Early Christian theologians like Tertullian and Augustine also expressed skepticism about integrating secular knowledge with religious beliefs, arguing that faith should take precedence over empirical inquiry.

6.1.2 The Renaissance and the Rise of Empirical Science

The Renaissance, a cultural movement spanning the 14th to 17th centuries, brought about a renewed interest in empirical methods of inquiry and classical sources of knowledge. This intellectual shift challenged the authority of the Catholic Church, which held considerable influence over the philosophical and scientific beliefs of the time.

Scientific advancements during this period, such as Copernicus's heliocentric model and Galileo's telescopic observations of the heavens, fueled the debate between religion and science. The Catholic Church held the geocentric model, with the Earth as the center of the universe, based on their interpretation of biblical passages. When faced with evidence supporting an alternative view of the cosmos, religious authorities rejected these findings, condemning Copernicus's and Galileo's theories as heretical.

The controversy surrounding these scientific developments led to an increasing gap between religious and scientific authority—an ideological divide that laid the groundwork for future episodes of religious and scientific strife.

6.1.3 The Enlightenment and the Scientific Revolution

As the 17th and 18th centuries saw the rise of the Enlightenment and the Scientific Revolution, religion and science continued their contentious interactions. Major scientific figures, such as Isaac Newton and Robert Boyle, held strong religious beliefs, often seeking to reconcile their scientific discoveries with their faith.

However, this period also witnessed an unprecedented growth in skepticism and secularism. Philosophers like David Hume and Denis Diderot questioned the legitimacy of religious doctrines and promoted the use of reason and empirical evidence as the basis of knowledge. The Enlightenment contributed to the rise of Deism, a belief system that rejected traditional religious teachings in favor of the idea of a rational creator that set the laws of nature and was uninvolved in the everyday workings of the universe.

6.1.4 Charles Darwin, Evolution, and the Modern Debate

Charles Darwin's groundbreaking publication of *On the Origin of Species* (1859) served as a catalyst for further conflict between religion and science. Darwin's evolutionary theory fundamentally challenged traditional religious beliefs of divine creation, proposing that species developed through the gradual process of natural selection.

As a result, Darwin faced opposition by religious institutions and figures who rejected the notion of evolution, viewing it as a threat to biblical authority. The tension between evolutionary theory and religious belief persists today, evident in the debates surrounding the teaching of evolution and intelligent design in public schools.

In recent years, the debate has widened to include other scientific fields, such as cosmology and neuroscience, which have implications for religious concepts of the origins of the universe and the nature of the human mind. These developments have sparked an ongoing dialogue about the respective roles of religion and science in human understanding and society.

6.2 Navigating the Philosophy of Non-Belief in the Face of Religion and Science

For atheists engaging with the complex relationship between religion and science, it is essential to approach the subject with an openness to dialogue and understanding. Recognizing that religious and scientific truths can coexist, albeit often at odds with each other, is an essential part of examining the world through an atheist lens.

There are many challenging questions that arise for atheists when considering the interplay of religious and scientific influences on human thought, knowledge, and culture. How do we balance the desire for empirical evidence and rational thinking with the recognition that religious beliefs hold deep meaning for much of humanity? Can the naturalistic explanations provided by science fully account for the range of human experiences, values, and aspirations that have often been framed through the lens of religious narratives?

Atheists who engage with the topic of religion versus science should be prepared to grapple with these questions, recognizing the diverse perspectives and experiences that inform our understanding of the world. Overall, by adopting an open-minded approach to education and dialogue, atheists can contribute to the ongoing pursuit of truth, wherever it may be found.

6.2 Exploring the Alleged Conflict Between Religion and Science

Throughout history, the relationship between religion and science has been a subject of intense debate and numerous discussions. For some people, these two areas of thought and belief appear to be in a constant state of conflict, with each one attempting to discredit and undermine the other. However, is such a conflict inherent in the nature of these disciplines, or is it instead a product of the various cultural, social, and historical contexts in which they have evolved? In this subsection, we will delve into the history of this alleged battle, consider the motivations behind the perpetuation of such a conflict, and examine whether the polarization between religion and science is inevitable, or if there could be a way to reconcile the two.

A Brief History of Religion and Science Encounters

Humans have long been in the pursuit of knowledge and answers to some fundamental questions regarding their existence and the natural world. While religion has developed over millennia to provide a spiritual and moral framework for understanding these questions, science has continually developed as a comprehensive method for gathering and interpreting empirical evidence derived from the natural world. As such, both religion and science seek to provide a framework for understanding aspects of our lives and the world around us.

However, the history of the encounter between religion and science is not always a tale of peace and cooperation. Amongst the most famous examples is the case of Galileo Galilei, who faced trial and imprisonment by the Catholic Church for his heliocentric views that contradicted official Church doctrine. The impact of this event on the perception of the relationship between religion and science cannot be overstated; it marked the beginning of an increasingly fraught journey in which both fields would come to be seen as adversaries.

But it is important to note that not every interaction between these two areas of study resulted in hostility or suppression. For instance, many scientist-clerics like Roger Bacon, Nicholas Copernicus, and Gregor Mendel made significant scientific discoveries while remaining deeply religious.

Perpetuating the Conflict: Factors and Motivations

Numerous factors have contributed to the perpetuation of the supposed conflict between religion and science, including the influence of cultural and historical contexts, the need to protect vested interests, and the desire for power and control.

On one hand, religious institutions have historically wielded considerable power and exerted substantial influence on various aspects of society, including the realm of science. Tensions arose when scientific findings or theories appeared to challenge religious doctrines or contradict traditional beliefs. For some religious institutions, maintaining the status quo was crucial to preserving their authority and influence; therefore, they adopted various strategies to suppress or discredit findings that were perceived as threatening.

Conversely, some proponents of science have been spurred on by similar motivations, seeking to frame religion as an irrational and antiquated system of belief that has no place in modern society. They argue that science is the only valid and objective means by which we can understand the natural world, often invoking Occam's razor and favoring atheistic interpretations of scientific findings.

However, this antagonistic stance sometimes overlooks the fact that religion and science answer fundamentally different questions and address distinct aspects of existence. While science seeks to understand the natural world by observing, experimenting, and providing empirical explanations, religion explores questions of purpose, meaning, and morality.

Is Reconciliation Possible?

The question of whether it is possible to reconcile religion and science is complex and multifaceted, involving not only theoretical considerations but also social and cultural factors. While there are undoubtedly areas of overlap and tension between these two domains of knowledge, it is important to recognize that each has its own unique methods, objectives, and limitations.

To facilitate a more productive dialogue between religion and science, it is important to maintain a sense of humility and open-mindedness. A willingness to listen, learn, and engage in constructive conversation can help to foster mutual understanding and respect. Furthermore, recognizing that there may be more than one valid perspective or interpretation of certain issues can lead to more fruitful exchanges and a richer understanding of the world in which we live.

In recent years, there has been a surge in interest in exploring the connections between science and spirituality. Some scientists and theologians are joining forces to develop an "integrative framework," which seeks to reconcile scientific findings with religious beliefs. This approach acknowledges that religion and science can coexist, complementing each other in providing different facets of our human understanding.

Ultimately, it is crucial to recognize that the perceived conflict between religion and science may be more a reflection of the human proclivity for competition and conflict than of any inherent incompatibility between these two great domains of human thought and exploration.

6.2. The Conflict Thesis: War between Religion and Science

The Conflict Thesis posits an intrinsic and inevitable opposition between religion and science. This idea can be traced back to the 19th century works of John William Draper and Andrew Dickson White. In Draper's "History of the Conflict between Religion and Science" (1874) and White's "A History of the Warfare of Science with Theology in Christendom" (1896), these authors argue that a historical struggle between scientific progress and religious dogma exists at the heart of our understanding of the world. They portray science as being in continuous conflict with religion, where scientific achievements were suppressed or attacked by the religious establishment. While this narrative has since been criticized and questioned by contemporary historians of science, it still offers a framework for understanding some of the tensions that may arise between religious and scientific perspectives.

6.2.1. Historical Conflicts

There are several key historical examples that are often cited by proponents of the Conflict Thesis to illustrate the struggle between religion and science:

- The most well-known case is the trial of **Galileo Galilei** in 1633. Galileo supported the heliocentric model of the universe (originally proposed by Copernicus), which contradicted the geocentric model sanctioned by the Catholic Church at the time. As a result, the Inquisition found him guilty of heresy, and he was placed under house arrest for the rest of his life.
- The story of **Giordano Bruno**, a 16th-century Dominican friar, is another famous example. Bruno advocated for a Copernican cosmology and an infinite universe, ideas that directly opposed the teachings of the Church. He was subsequently burned at the stake for heresy in 1600.
- The publication of **Charles Darwin's** "On the Origin of Species" in 1859, advocating for the theory of evolution by natural selection, also sparked significant religious debate. In the infamous Scopes "Monkey Trial" of 1925, a high school teacher in the United States was charged with violating state law by teaching evolution in a public school. This case became a battleground between religious fundamentalists, who argued for a literal interpretation of the Bible, and proponents of scientific modernism.

6.2.2. Epistemological Differences

The Conflict Thesis is supported by the argument that the epistemological foundations of religion and science fundamentally differ. Science thrives on observation, evidence, experimentation, and falsifiability, where new ideas can only be accepted after rigorous scrutiny and testing. The scientific method is designed to weed out false ideas so that we're left with the most accurate representations of the natural world.

In contrast, religious knowledge is frequently grounded in revelation, authority, and sacred texts. Many religious claims cannot be subjected to empirical testing, thereby making them immune to refutation. This way of acquiring knowledge can sometimes result in unjustified certainties, which could undermine scientific inquiry.

6.2.3. Philosophical Debates

The Conflict Thesis also extends to several ongoing debates in the philosophy of science and religion:

- **Miracles** - Science is built on predictability and natural laws, while religious faith often relies on the concept of miracles. Miracles, by definition, are violations of natural laws and can be seen as at odds with the scientific worldview.
- **Methodological Naturalism** - This position suggests that science can and should only deal with natural phenomena and not delve into supernatural explanations. Inherent in this perspective is the belief that there is no place for religious or supernatural claims within scientific methodology.
- **Demarcation Problem** - How do we distinguish between science and non-science (or pseudoscience)? This issue implies that there is an

inherent incompatibility between scientific knowledge and religious or metaphysical claims.

Despite the historical and philosophical tensions suggested by the Conflict Thesis, it is crucial to note that many historians and philosophers reject this binary view of religion and science. They argue that the relationship between the two is much more complex and nuanced, with examples of cooperation, dialogue, and even integration throughout history.

Regardless of whether one subscribes to the Conflict Thesis, it remains an important starting point for discussing the interactions between religion and science in modern society. It prompts us to consider the implications of approaching the world through different lenses and explore the value of fostering a mutual respect for these diverse perspectives in our pursuit of truth.

7. Navigating a Religious World as an Atheist: Society and Culture

7.3 Learning to Coexist with Religious Believers

A significant aspect of being an atheist in a religious world is learning how to coexist, engage in conversations, and maintain relationships. Most societies have religious majorities, and as an atheist, it is crucial to find a balance between asserting our beliefs and respecting those of believers. The following subsections of this chapter discuss empathy, understanding, and dialog, all of which can help us engage effectively with the religious world.

7.3.1 Building Empathy

Like any deep-rooted belief, religious convictions can serve as a bastion for many people, providing them with a sense of solace, community, and answers to life's big questions. Understanding this aspect of religion can help us empathize with believers and lend credence to the saying, "You don't have to agree with someone to understand them."

To build empathy, we must actively be aware of our emotional reactions to people's beliefs, even if we disagree with them. For instance, try stepping into their shoes and consider why they might feel the strength of their convictions. Empathy not only allows us to forge a common ground between opposing views but to build a strong rapport with other people as well.

7.3.2 Respectful Communication

Engaging in conversations about religion and atheism can be challenging. The goal should be to assert our position without belittling the believer's stance, generating animosity or condescension. A few pointers to facilitate respectful communication include:

1. **Listen carefully**: Make a conscious effort to listen actively to what the other person is saying, and avoid interrupting them. This can help avoid misinterpretation and demonstrate a genuine desire to understand their point of view.
2. **Focus on ideas, not individuals**: When considering differing opinions, it is important to separate the idea from the person holding it. This allows for a more open and nuanced discussion of the topic, and avoids resorting to personal attacks.

3. **Acknowledge commonalities**: Recognizing shared values and concerns can foster mutual understanding and form the basis for constructive dialogue. For example, one might acknowledge a shared desire to understand the nature of the universe.
4. **Avoid aggressive language**: Choosing words carefully can prevent discussions from becoming heated or accusatory. Avoid making sweeping generalizations, as they can alienate rather than engage.

7.3.3 Engaging in Interfaith Dialog

Participating in interfaith dialogues and events can facilitate a better understanding of the reasons for personal faith, furthering our ability to engage in empathetic and respectful conversations. Additionally, these dialogues can provide opportunities for atheist advocacy and foster relationships with like-minded individuals.

While attending interfaith events, be prepared to present atheism as a legitimate, well-formed worldview. This can be achieved by highlighting ethical and philosophical secular values, such as the importance of evidence-based reasoning and the development of a moral compass independent of religious teachings.

7.3.4 Maintaining Relationships

Navigating relationships with religious family members or friends can sometimes be tricky. Honest, open communication and mutual respect are key factors in fostering enduring relationships that can weather ideological differences. Be careful not to impose your beliefs on others, and similarly, do not tolerate proselytization from religious individuals. It is important to establish boundaries for what is and isn't acceptable in discussions about personal beliefs.

In conclusion, navigating a religious world as an atheist involves building empathy, respectful communication, engaging in interfaith dialogues, and maintaining relationships amidst differing beliefs. Approaching others with kindness, understanding, and a willingness to engage in meaningful conversations can bridge the divide between atheists and believers, contributing to a richer, more inclusive society.

Navigating Religious Traditions and Celebrations

As an atheist, you may find yourself living in a world that revolves around religious traditions and celebrations. These events might include Christmas, Easter, Ramadan, Diwali, Hanukkah, or other culturally significant milestones often rooted in religious beliefs. It is essential to develop an understanding and appreciation for these traditions, even if you do not personally subscribe to the beliefs that inspired them.

Understanding the Significance of Religious Holidays

To begin, it is essential to understand the significance and meanings behind religious holidays. As an atheist, you may not believe in miracles, divine interventions, or other supernatural occurrences that form the basis of many religious celebrations. However, you can still acknowledge and respect the cultural and historical significance of these events for the people who do believe in them.

For example, Christmas, celebrated worldwide by Christians as the birth of Jesus Christ, is also recognized as a time of love, happiness, and unity. While you might not believe in a divine birth, you may still choose to participate in the customs surrounding the holiday by expressing love and gratitude to those around you or by giving and receiving gifts. By understanding the context and customs of religious holidays, you can participate in a more meaningful way and bridge the gap between your own atheism and the beliefs of others.

Respecting the Beliefs of Others

Respect for the beliefs of others is at the core of navigating a religious world as an atheist. This means not belittling or ridiculing religious customs, practices, or beliefs, even if you don't agree with them or find them logical. You do not have to adopt these beliefs yourself – indeed, doing so would likely be disingenuous and futile – yet you should acknowledge that other people have the right to hold them without interference or judgment.

Try to empathize with people who hold religious beliefs and celebrate religious rituals. Many individuals find solace, hope, and inspiration in their faith, which may help them cope with life's challenges and uncertainties. While your worldview may differ, the ability to empathize with others' experiences and convictions will enable you to engage more compassionately and effectively in conversations around religion and spirituality.

Individual Choices in Participating in Customs and Rituals

As an atheist, you have the freedom to determine your level of involvement in religious customs and rituals. Some atheists choose to abstain from these activities altogether, while others engage in family traditions or attend religious ceremonies to show support for loved ones. Each decision is valid, as long as it is made with self-reflection, respect, and honesty.

Regardless of your decision, try to communicate openly with your friends, family, and community to minimize misunderstandings and conflicts. Share your rationale for your choices with respect and understanding, and listen to other people's perspectives and experiences. Remember that you can gracefully decline invitations to religious ceremonies or politely exit conversations that challenge your beliefs, as long as you approach such situations with respect and understanding.

Seeking Out Other Atheists or Non-religious Communities

Navigating a religious world as an atheist can be challenging, particularly during religious holidays or events. It can sometimes feel lonely or isolating, especially if you are surrounded by people who do not share your beliefs. For this reason, it may be helpful to seek like-minded individuals or communities that can offer support, understanding, and camaraderie.

Explore local atheist, humanist, or skeptical organizations, or look for online communities on social media or discussion boards. These spaces provide opportunities to connect with fellow atheists, share experiences and insights, and engage in open conversations about what it means to live as a non-believer in a religious world.

Conclusion

Navigating a religious world as an atheist requires understanding, empathy, and respect—both for yourself and for others. By appreciating the cultural and historical significance of religious holidays and traditions, asserting your own beliefs respectfully and empathetically, and seeking support from like-minded individuals, you can lead a fulfilling and inclusive life as an atheist in a predominantly religious world. After all, human connections and shared experiences are vital to our well-being, regardless of the beliefs that guide our lives.

Navigating a Religious World as an Atheist: Society and Culture

Understanding the Sociocultural Landscape of Religion

As an atheist, it is essential to gain a comprehensive understanding of the various religious beliefs and practices that pervade today's world. This involves not only grasping the basic tenets and underlying philosophies of major religions but also examining how they shape culture, politics, social dynamics, and individual behaviors. By appreciating the breadth and depth of religious influences on society, atheists can engage meaningfully with religious individuals and navigate complex, faith-based issues with sensitivity and awareness.

Exploring Common Religious Practices, Values, and Norms

At the heart of most religious traditions are fundamental values that often dictate acceptable behaviors, beliefs, and practices. Some of these values—such as compassion, empathy, and nonviolence—are universally commendable, transcending specific religious or nonreligious belief systems. Other aspects, such as dietary restrictions, dress codes, or suggested prayers and rituals, may be unique to particular faiths. A thorough understanding of these norms allows atheists to interact respectfully with individuals from diverse religious backgrounds and appreciate the unique perspectives inherent in their worldviews.

Recognizing the Role of Religion in Identity Formation

Religion can have a significant impact on how individuals define and perceive their own identities. This may involve a sense of belonging to a particular religious group, adherence to role expectations within that group, or incorporation of specific religious tenets into one's moral and ethical framework. For atheists, it is crucial to empathize with the central role that religion may play in other people's lives and to appreciate that such commitments can be deeply intertwined with personal identity. By respecting believers' rights to define themselves in relation to their faith, atheists can promote a tolerant and empathetic society in which a diversity of religious and secular identities can coexist harmoniously.

Acknowledging Religion's Influence on Cultural Traditions

Religion has shaped innumerable cultural practices and traditions worldwide, from artistic expressions and architecture to culinary and social customs. As atheists, it is essential to recognize that many of the rituals, symbols, and celebrations that permeate contemporary society have religious origins, regardless of whether they have been secularized over time. Appreciating the cultural legacy of religious traditions allows atheists not only to understand the richness of human history and experience but also to partake in these cultural expressions and share in the joy and meaning that they can bring to individuals and communities.

Engaging in Respectful and Informed Dialogue with Religious Individuals

One of the challenges that atheists may face in a religious world is navigating conversations about religion, particularly when discussing personal beliefs, organized religion, or broader spiritual topics. It is vital for atheists to approach such discussions with openness, curiosity, and respect, endeavoring to learn from religious believers and share their philosophical perspectives in a mutually enriching dialogue. This means avoiding condescending, dismissive, or aggressive attitudes that may alienate others or create unnecessary tensions. Atheists can benefit from exploring the nuances of religious thought, while offering their perspective on ethics, meaning, and purpose in life without presupposing religious belief.

Addressing Discrimination and Stereotyping

Unfortunately, atheists sometimes encounter discrimination or prejudice due to misperceptions or lack of understanding about their beliefs. This prejudice may manifest in the form of discrimination, harassment, or bias, particularly in areas where religious faith is a dominant cultural force. Atheists can help mitigate these challenges by dispelling common stereotypes, promoting awareness of atheism's philosophical foundations, and advocating for fair treatment of individuals regardless of their beliefs. Additionally, atheists must be committed to rejecting and confronting discrimination based on religious beliefs, upholding the value of diversity and supporting a society in which all individuals are respected and their rights protected.

Embracing Community and Building Support Networks

Although religious communities often provide substantial social, emotional, and spiritual support for believers, atheists can also form and engage in thriving communities united by shared values, goals, or interests. These communities might include secular humanist organizations, atheist or freethinker groups, or local clubs focused on intellectual or social pursuits. By developing strong social ties within these networks, atheists can gain camaraderie, emotional support, and a sense of belonging, enhancing their well-being and cultivating resilience in the face of religious pressures or challenges.

In summary, navigating a religious world as an atheist involves understanding and appreciating the multi-faceted role of religion in society and culture while maintaining one's own philosophical convictions. This approach enables atheists to engage meaningfully with religious individuals and communities, confront discrimination, and lead fulfilling lives that contribute to a pluralistic, tolerant world.

8. Atheism in Literature and Art: Creative Expressions of Non-Belief

The Intersection of Atheism, Literature, and Art

Throughout history, creative expressions have been used to communicate and dialogue with a wider audience about an infinite variety of subjects. These creative expressions include the domains of literature and the visual arts, which have been utilized as vehicles to express thoughts, emotions, and philosophies. Atheism, as a fascinating and profound philosophical stance, has seen its share of representation in both of these domains.

In this section, we will explore a variety of authors and artists who have employed their creative talents to express atheistic themes and ideas. This exploration will showcase how atheism can be represented in fiction, poetry, painting, and other visual arts. By delving into these works, we can gain a deeper understanding of atheism, and appreciate the myriad ways in which it has been expressed throughout human history.

Fiction

Atheism has found a strong voice in literature since ancient times. Novels, plays and poems have often been the perfect medium for expressing critique, reflection and exploration of religion, faith and the notion of god. Below are some outstanding examples of books featuring atheist themes and characters:

1. *The Brothers Karamazov* by Fyodor Dostoevsky: This 1880 novel offers a deep philosophical exploration of faith, doubt, and reason. While Dostoevsky himself was religious, his character Ivan Karamazov offers a

powerful voice for atheistic ideas, particularly through his famous poem "The Grand Inquisitor."

2. *Candide* by Voltaire: This 1759 satire attacks religious institutions and features the eponymous protagonist embracing reason over religion as he loses faith in God through his various misadventures.
3. *Brave New World* by Aldous Huxley: This 1932 dystopian novel is set in a world where organized religion has been replaced by worship of Henry Ford and science. As the inhabitants of this society struggle to find meaning in life without religious belief, Huxley offers a critique of an atheistic society's potential pitfalls.

Poetry

Poetry has long been a favored tool for expressing philosophical ideas, and atheism is no exception. The condensed language of poetry enables some atheist poets to communicate their disbelief clearly and powerfully:

1. Percy Bysshe Shelley: This 19th-century English poet was a vocal atheist, penning works like "The Necessity of Atheism" and the epic "Prometheus Unbound," in which he champions free will and human potential over the constraints of organized religion.
2. Emily Dickinson: While all of her poetry may not express an overt atheist viewpoint, Dickinson's work often challenges religious orthodoxy and offers complex examinations of faith and doubt.
3. Philip Larkin: The 20th-century English poet's work is marked by a profound skepticism of religion, with many poems questioning the existence of God and the role of faith in human life.

Visual Arts

Artists throughout history have employed their visual talents to explore atheistic themes, both overtly and subtly:

1. Francisco Goya: The 18th-century Spanish painter and printmaker's work often exhibited a deep skepticism of the Catholic Church and religion in general. His powerful *Los Caprichos* and *Disasters of War* series critique superstition and religious violence.
2. Max Ernst: The 20th-century German painter and sculptor played an influential role in both the Dada and Surrealist movements, which often critiqued religion as a manifestation of human irrationality.
3. Frida Kahlo: The 20th-century Mexican painter was a self-proclaimed atheist, and her work often included atheist iconography, rejecting religious traditions and exploring themes of self-empowerment and personal agency.

Conclusion

The creative expressions of atheism in literature and art provide a powerful mirror through which we can explore our own convictions, address our doubts, and challenge our beliefs. By examining the works of authors and artists who have grappled with the questions of faith, doubt, and disbelief, we can begin to develop a more comprehensive understanding of the rich history and diversity of atheistic thought.

Ultimately, art transcends borders and languages, offering a unique and profound perspective on that which binds and divides us. Atheism in literature and art bears testament to the ongoing quest for human understanding and liberation from dogmatic thinking, and it serves as a reminder that art is a vehicle powerful enough to take on even the most sacred ideas.

8.2 The Power of Imagination: Depicting a Godless World in Literature and Art

8.2.1 Atheism in Literature

Throughout history, literature has played a crucial role in challenging prevailing religious thought and exploring the implications of a world without gods. Writers of varying literary styles and time periods have presented fascinating perspectives on the potential of a godless world. While some authors may have been atheists themselves, others may not have explicitly identified as such; but their works remain valuable in presenting alternative viewpoints on the existence and nature of God. Let us delve into a few major literary works that explore atheism and its implications.

8.2.1.1 Prometheus Unbound by Percy Bysshe Shelley

As an archetype of resistance against traditional systems of religious authority and power, Prometheus has signified humanity's rebellious spirit since the days of ancient Greece. Percy Bysshe Shelley's 'Prometheus Unbound' is a poetic drama that retells the myth of Prometheus, modifying the story to depict the ultimate triumph of humanity over divine tyranny.

Shelley himself was a committed atheist and social reformer, and he employed the figure of Prometheus as a symbol for the possibility of humanity's freedom from religious orthodoxy. The poem's portrayal of Zeus – as a cruel, unyielding torturer who ultimately falls from power – serves to criticize the idea of an omnipotent, benevolent deity. Ultimately, the poem presents an optimistic vision of a world in which humanity, unshackled from the constraints of divine determinism, can forge its destiny and create a just, egalitarian society.

8.2.1.2 The Brothers Karamazov by Fyodor Dostoevsky

Fyodor Dostoevsky's magnum opus, 'The Brothers Karamazov,' weaves intricate moral, spiritual, and philosophical questions throughout the intense interplay of its vividly drawn characters. Among the novel's central themes is an exploration of God's existence and His role in human suffering. Through the character of Ivan Karamazov, a rationalist and atheist, Dostoevsky presents a powerful critique of religious belief.

In the infamous "Grand Inquisitor" chapter, Ivan conjures a parable of Jesus returning to confront the Spanish Inquisition, illustrating how the Church itself had corrupted Christ's teachings to wield control over humanity. He also challenges the concept of a loving God by pointing to the unbearable suffering of children. While Dostoevsky himself was a devout Christian, his work allows readers to ponder the implications of an alternative, godless worldview on morality and personal responsibility.

8.2.1.3 The Stranger by Albert Camus

The existentialist classic 'The Stranger' by Albert Camus explores the futility of seeking meaning and rationality in a chaotic, indifferent universe. The novel's protagonist, Meursault, an emotionally detached and amoral man, experiences a series of events that force him to confront the absurdity of existence. Constructed on the foundation of Nietzsche's pronouncement of God's death, Camus' assertion of the absurdity of life's meaning has links to atheism.

Through Meursault's character, Camus emphasizes the indifference of the universe, wherein human beings must create their sense of purpose and morality without relying on supernatural guidance. Atheistic existentialism pervades the novel, highlighting the personal freedom and responsibility individuals must bear in the absence of divine authority. This thought-provoking work encourages readers to explore the implications of a world void of predetermined meaning and rules, instigating an internal dialogue about atheism and existentialism.

8.2.2 Atheism in Art

Art, much like literature, affords an invaluable medium for expressing and evaluating atheistic themes and ideas. Throughout history, artists have used their skills to challenge religious beliefs, offer support for atheism, or merely explore the ramifications of a world without gods. Here, we highlight two influential artistic movements that espoused or engaged with atheistic ideas.

8.2.2.1 The Enlightenment: Emphasizing Reason Over Religion

The Enlightenment, a movement from the 17th to the 19th century, prioritized rational thought and skepticism, whittling away at the formerly unbending authority of the Church. Scientific advancements and a burgeoning intellectual curiosity led to an increased appreciation for empirical evidence, underscoring the contrast between reason and religious dogma.

While some artists and philosophers of this era may not have been overt atheists, their questioning and critique of religious power allowed for a new openness in exploring atheism. Art during the Enlightenment often focused on the human intellect and the potential inherent in science and human achievement, challenging the more traditional, religious-based themes.

8.2.2.2 Dadaism and Surrealism: Rebellion Against Orthodoxy

The Dada and Surrealist movements, born from the chaos and devastation of World War I, explicitly challenged traditional norms and dogma, including religious orthodoxy. With their subversive and unconventional approach to art, Dadaists and Surrealists sought to redefine human values in the aftermath of the war, aiming to distance themselves from the established structures deemed responsible for the conflict, including religion.

In doing so, many artists within these movements rejected the idea of divine intervention, creating works that reveled in absurdity, unreason, and chaos. By dismantling the confines of religious hierarchies and expectations, they opened up space for considering non-traditional belief systems, including atheism.

8.2.3 Conclusion

Atheism in literature and art plays a vital role in exploring, challenging, and expanding on themes present within religious narratives. Through their mastery of word and stroke, these creative minds have captured the imagination of countless individuals. Their works encourage readers and viewers to question traditional dogma, analyze alternative world views, and ponder the profound implications that come with a life devoid of supernatural deities. The scope of atheism in literature and art is vast and multifaceted, providing fertile ground for individuals to engage in a deeply personal dialogue with their beliefs, skepticism, and the fundamental nature of existence.

8.2 The Atheist's Voice: A Journey Through Literary Works and Artistic Endeavors

For generations, atheists have woven their thoughts and beliefs into the fabric of literature and art. These creative expressions of non-belief have not only allowed them to espouse their worldview but also capture the essence of what it means to be an atheist in a predominantly religious world. This section delves into the history, various forms, and impact of atheism in literature and art, from novels and poetry to paintings, sculptures, and even cinema.

8.2.1 Early Expressions of Non-Belief

As far back as the ancient Greeks, skeptics and atheists have made their voices heard through the written word in both philosophical texts and narratives. Perhaps the most prominent example from this era is the pre-Socratic philosopher Democritus, who rejected the notion of divine beings in favor of a materialistic view of the world. His "atomistic" theory suggested that the universe is only composed of indivisible, minute particles called atoms, which governed by natural laws instead of having a supernatural influence.

In ancient Rome, the poet Lucretius penned the philosophical epic poem *De Rerum Natura* ("On the Nature of Things"), building upon Democritus's ideas and arguing for a purely mechanistic cosmos. Lucretius explored themes that could be seen as atheistic or at least skeptical, such as the non-existence of an immortal soul and the futility of religion.

During the Renaissance, skepticism grew due in large part to the exposure and dissemination of classical texts that had been lost during the Middle Ages. One notable figure of this period, Machiavelli, wrote in his work *The Prince* that religion was a tool used by rulers to control the masses. His secular and pragmatic views reflected a shift toward less religiously centered thought.

8.2.2 The Age of Enlightenment and Beyond

As the Age of Enlightenment dawned in the 17th and 18th centuries, so too did the rise of rationalism and empiricism. Skepticism toward religion and its institutions continued to grow, leading to an increased presence of atheistic themes in literature and art.

Notable thinkers such as David Hume, Jean-Jacques Rousseau, and Immanuel Kant grappled with questions of religion, morality, and the nature of the divine through their writing. These philosophers expressed doubts concerning the evidence for and necessity of a god, contributing to an intellectual climate that saw the deconstruction of traditional religious narratives.

In the world of fiction, Voltaire's *Candide* satirically ridicules the concept of "Panglossian optimism," which is the idea that "all is for the best" in a divinely ruled universe. His contemporary, Denis Diderot, was a staunch atheist who dared to challenge the Christian church openly in his work. In *The Nun*, Diderot questioned the motivations and consequences of religious institutions, while *Rameau's Nephew* openly mocked religious hypocrisy.

8.2.3 Romanticism, Realism, and the Critique of Faith

Moving into the 19th century, the Romantic era saw a shift in focus from reason to emotion and individualism. Some authors, such as Percy Bysshe Shelley, used this as an opportunity to explore atheism within a deeply personal context. Shelley's work, including his famous Defense of Poetry, contained arguments against the existence of a supreme being and advocated for a more secular, humanistic view of the world.

With the rise of realism and naturalism in literature, more writers began to question the role of religion in their societies. In works such as Gustave Flaubert's *Madame Bovary* and Émile Zola's *Germinal*, the ways in which religious beliefs stifled personal growth and contributed to human suffering were depicted with brutal honesty.

8.2.4 Modernism and the Twentieth Century

In the twentieth century, the atheistic voice in literature continued to evolve, influenced by the widespread disillusionment caused by two world wars and an increasingly scientific worldview. Authors such as Vladimir Nabokov, F. Scott Fitzgerald, and Ernest Hemingway called into question the relevance of faith in an era marked by insecurity and questioning.

One of the most potent examples of atheist literature in the twentieth century can be found in Albert Camus's *The Stranger*. A landmark existentialist novel, it tells the story of

Meursault, a man who remains indifferent to the world around him, including its religious customs and expectations.

In poetry, the work of Philip Larkin stands as a prime example of the atheistic voice in verse. His collections, such as *The Whitsun Weddings* and *High Windows*, are marked by themes of skeptical inquiry and expressions of religious doubt.

8.2.5 Atheism in Visual Arts and Cinema

In addition to literature, atheism and skepticism have found their way into visual arts and cinema. Painters such as Francis Bacon, Rene Magritte, and Pablo Picasso have incorporated themes questioning religion and the nature of existence, as seen in Picasso's *Guernica* and Magritte's *The Treachery of Images*.

In cinema, atheistic themes have been explored in films such as Ingmar Bergman's *The Seventh Seal*, which tells the story of a knight questioning the existence of God during the plague-ridden days of the Middle Ages. Similarly, Luis Buñuel's *The Exterminating Angel* satirizes the failings and hypocrisy of Catholicism, while Stanley Kubrick's *2001: A Space Odyssey* offers a vision of humanity transcending its origins without divine assistance.

From ancient times to the present day, atheism has found its voice through a wide range of literary works and artistic expressions. This rich history highlights the evolving ways in which non-believers have grappled with questions of existence, morality, and the role religion has played in human history. For both authors and artists, these creative endeavors have provided a platform to express their beliefs, share their insights, and offer an alternative perspective on the way we understand our world.

9. The Future of Atheism: Religion, Secularism, and Global Trends

9.2 Global Trends Shaping the Future of Atheism

Atheism, as an intellectual and philosophical position, has remained a persistent feature of human thought for centuries. However, it's essential to recognize that atheism does not remain stable over time but rather evolves, just as religious beliefs do. By examining the global trends that have an impact on religious and secular beliefs, we can gain insight into the future of atheism and its potential directions.

9.2.1 Demographic Changes and the Rise of the "Nones"

One of the most significant global trends affecting religion is the rise of the "Nones" – people who identify as having no religion or no particular religious affiliation. The number of Nones has increased dramatically in recent years, with some countries – such as the United States, Canada, and various European countries – experiencing a noticeable decline in the percentage of the population that identifies as religious.

This trend has important implications for the future of atheism. As fewer people identify with a particular religious tradition or practice, atheism and secularism become appealing alternatives. The rise of the Nones provides a fertile ground for the growth and dissemination of atheist ideas, allowing for further interaction between religious and non-religious communities.

9.2.2 Technological Developments and the Impact on Religious Belief

Advancements in technology are also shaping the future of atheism. Increased access to information about atheism, whether through online communities, forums, or social media platforms, has facilitated the spread of atheistic ideas and fostered a sense of solidarity among atheists around the world.

Additionally, scientific advancements are increasingly providing explanations for phenomena that were once attributed to the divine, reducing the reliance on religious explanations for understanding the world. As technological and scientific progress continues, we can expect that atheism will become an increasingly popular worldview, as it offers a viable and rational explanation of the world that is grounded in empirical evidence.

9.2.3 The Shift Towards Personal Spirituality and Individualism

There is a growing trend of people being more interested in personal spirituality than in adhering to specific religious doctrines or institutions. This shift towards individualism and personal spirituality is likely to continue shaping the landscape of religious belief and promote the further diversification of religious expression.

The move towards personal spirituality allows for the incorporation of atheistic and secular perspectives within this diverse tapestry, as individuals may adopt a mix of ideas and practices, such as secular Buddhism or humanist ethics. This shift may help destigmatize atheism and contribute to a more accepting and pluralistic society, where a range of beliefs and worldviews can coexist peacefully.

9.2.4 The Future Role of Religion in Public Life and Politics

The question of whether religion should play a role in public life and policymaking is a deeply divisive one, especially in countries with a history of political secularism. As atheism becomes a mainstream worldview and the Nones continue to grow in number, the debate around the proper role of religion in society is likely to become even more pronounced.

The future of atheism might play a crucial role in shaping these debates, as secular and non-religious voices argue for a continued separation between religious institutions and state apparatus. Furthermore, the rise of secular activism and advocacy may change the landscape of public discourse, pushing for a more secular and pluralistic society where religious and non-religious perspectives can coexist while maintaining distinct domains.

9.2.5 The Interplay of Religious Conflict and Atheism

In regions where religious conflicts are sadly prevalent, the consequences of these hostilities may shape the perception of religion and foster atheism. As religious extremism and violence continue to affect societies worldwide, individuals may turn away from religion and seek solace in atheist or secularist ideals that advocate for a more peaceful and rational engagement with different worldviews.

While atheism itself does not guarantee a more harmonious world, the future of atheism may well depend on how it is framed in contrast to religious conflict. By promoting a secular approach to conflict resolution that is inclusive and respectful of diverse perspectives, atheism could lead to the creation of a more peaceful world.

In conclusion, the future of atheism is shaped by various global trends, including demographic changes, technological developments, and the evolving role of religion in public life. As these trends continue to unfold, it is crucial for atheists and non-religious individuals to engage with these changes and participate in open dialogues with religious communities, fostering mutual understanding and promoting a pluralistic society that respects diverse perspectives.

9.2 The Atheist's Handbook: Exploring the Philosophy of Non-Belief:

The Future of Atheism: Religion, Secularism, and Global Trends

As we have explored throughout this book, atheism is not merely the absence of belief in God, but a rich and diverse philosophical tradition that has grown and evolved over time. It is a critical, inquisitive approach to the world, rooted in rational skepticism and a determination to follow the evidence wherever it leads. In this chapter, we will look ahead to the future of atheism, exploring the key trends shaping religion, secularism, and our broader global society.

We will discuss how the atheist movement as a whole is changing and what this means for the lives of individuals who identify as atheists.

9.2.1 The Changing Religious Landscape

One crucial factor in the future of atheism is how religion itself is changing. Traditionally, atheism has defined itself in opposition to theism—the belief in one or more gods. As a result, the decline or transformation of religious belief has significant implications for atheism's role within society.

We are currently witnessing a remarkable shift in the global religious landscape. In many parts of the world, particularly in North America and Western Europe, we see a decline in traditional religious adherence. Studies show an increasing number of people identifying as non-religious, or "nones," often described as those who answer "none" when asked about their religious affiliation. While some of these "nones" might still maintain a belief in a higher power or identify as spiritual, this trend represents a significant shift in religious identification.

On the other hand, some regions of the world, particularly in Africa and Asia, are witnessing a growth in religious adherence. This trend is particularly notable within Islam, which is projected to be the fastest growing major religion over the next few decades. What this means for the future of atheism is complex, as global religious dynamics will continue to shift and evolve, influencing political, social, and cultural landscapes.

9.2.2 The Role of Secularism

Another essential question for the future of atheism is the role of secularism in global society. By secularism, we mean the separation of religion and religious institutions from government and public affairs. In many ways, secularism can be seen as a framework that enables atheism to flourish, as it ensures that religious beliefs do not dominate public policy, creating room for diverse beliefs and opinions.

Secularism has been a central aspect of the atheist movement, with many campaigners arguing for church-state separation, the end of religious exemptions within the law, and the secularization of public education. In recent years, we have seen significant progress in these areas, with the establishment of secular policies and the decline of religious influence in certain areas of public life.

However, it is important to recognize that secularism is not synonymous with atheism. While secularism provides a space for atheism to exist alongside various religious beliefs, it does not inherently privilege atheism over any religious perspective. It aims at neutrality, recognizing and protecting the rights of all individuals regardless of their belief system. For atheism to thrive under secularism, it will need to continue promoting its philosophical ideas and engaging in constructive dialogue with people from diverse perspectives.

9.2.3 Global Ethics and Humanism

Another key aspect of the future of atheism is the development of global ethics and the broader humanist movement. Humanism is a philosophical outlook that emphasizes the moral value of human beings, grounded in reason, experience, and empathy, rather than relying on religious or supernatural explanations.

Many atheists identify with humanism, with some even arguing that humanism offers a more comprehensive positive ethical worldview that moves beyond a simple rejection of theism. In this sense, the future of atheism might involve an increasingly close relationship between the atheist and humanist movements, as both work to promote a rational, evidence-based approach to ethics and morality.

The development of global ethics will involve engaging with a diverse range of perspectives and cultural traditions, recognizing that the experiences and values of people from different backgrounds can inform our shared ethical journeys. This inclusive approach is necessary for atheism to remain a relevant force in the coming decades.

9.2.4 Atheism's Role in a World of Diversity

Finally, the future of atheism must also consider its role within an increasingly diverse and interconnected world. As society becomes more globalized, people from vastly different cultural and religious backgrounds will come into closer contact with one another, posing new challenges and opportunities for interfaith dialogue and engagement.

For atheism to continue to develop as a vibrant philosophical tradition, it must be willing to engage in productive conversations with other perspectives, particularly, if it wants to remain relevant and contribute positively to the evolving human story. This will require that atheists maintain an inquisitive, open-minded attitude, recognizing that wisdom and insight can be found across different cultures and spiritual traditions.

Moreover, the atheist movement must also consider how it can more effectively reach out to underrepresented communities and create inclusive spaces that welcome people from diverse backgrounds. Historically, atheism has tended to be more popular among white, male, and highly educated demographics. For atheism to continue to grow and flourish, it will need to make a concerted effort to foster a more inclusive and diverse movement.

In conclusion, the future of atheism is uncertain, shaped by shifting religious, secular, and ethical landscapes. As we navigate these complex global trends, it will be vital for the atheist movement to engage with diverse perspectives and strive to promote a more global and inclusive vision of human flourishing. The future of atheism is one that explores the vast possibilities of human inquiry, ethics, and dialogue, without fear of the unknown, but rather with the passion for understanding and embracing our shared human story.

9.1 Religion, Secularism, and Global Trends: Delving into the World's Collective Conscience

The future of atheism, similar to the evolution of religious beliefs, is affected by various factors such as globalization, technological advancements, political climate, and social progress. As with any ideology, atheism's place in society has never been stagnant – it constantly adapts and fluctuates in response to the ever-changing landscape of the world. This chapter delves into the different facets of secular growth, religion's role, and the emergence of global trends that influence their trajectories. It discusses what may lie ahead for atheism and how it can sustain itself as a rational, ethical alternative.

9.1.1 Globalization and its Role in Shaping Religious and Secular Beliefs

Globalization has brought forth an interconnected and interdependent world, where ideas and ideologies are freely exchanged, discussed, and challenged. This constant exposure to varying perspectives has played a critical role in shaping religious and secular beliefs around the globe.

The spread of atheism is no exception – it has exponentially increased with the exchange of ideas and the intermingling of cultures. Globalization has provided people the opportunity to explore other religious and non-religious philosophies, ultimately leading to a broader understanding, tolerance, and even acceptance of divergent beliefs.

However, globalization can also entail competition and, consequently, conflict. In response, religious institutions have evolved their practices and doctrines to address these challenges. For instance, some religious organizations have altered their ideologies to be more inclusive and accepting of modern lifestyles, resulting in the emergence of LGBTQ-friendly churches and evolving stances on gender equality.

In consequence, the world is experiencing a never-ending back-and-forth between religious and secular ideas. As religious ideologies are more freely expressed in society, the secular worldview seeks to counterbalance through promoting reasoning, skepticism, and evidence-based thinking, resulting in a tug-of-war struggle for the collective conscience of the world.

9.1.2 The Rise of Religious "Nones" and Freethinkers

A noteworthy and relatively recent phenomenon is the rise of individuals identifying as religious "nones" – people who are not affiliated with any particular religion or belief system, yet may still describe themselves as spiritual or agnostic. This category includes both atheists and agnostics, along with those who are simply disenchanted or disconnected from organized religion.

The number of religious nones has rapidly grown in the past few decades, especially in highly developed and secularized countries. A major factor behind this increase is the recognition and protection of individual liberties and freedoms. People who previously felt pressure to conform to religious traditions, but did not internally resonate with such beliefs, are increasingly finding solace in atheism or secularism.

The proliferation of information and communication via the Internet has made it easier for freethinkers to explore alternative worldviews and learn about atheism. Online forums, blogs, and social networking sites have created easily accessible spaces for honest debate and exchange pertaining to religious beliefs and doubts.

This trend is likely to continue as societies around the world face the realities of increasing diversity and the need for accepting different beliefs on both religious and secular fronts. This could lead to further growth and acknowledgment of atheist and agnostic individuals within communities.

9.1.3 The Potential Impact of Artificial Intelligence and Technological Advancements on Atheism

The many advancements that technological innovation brings about carry serious implications on morality, ethics, and belief systems. With artificial intelligence (AI) and automation becoming increasingly integrated into human lives, there are significant questions about how these innovations will affect human interactions with religion.

AI and robotics raise various ethical and moral concerns, as the traditional ideas of morality and ethics are posited to have stemmed from religious doctrines. Despite AI systems having the capacity to outperform humans in various tasks and functions, they do not hold innate moral values. This discrepancy raises a debate about ethics: Is morality solely derived from the divine, or can it be programmed into a machine?

Discussions centering on AI development are expected to challenge existing religious beliefs, further urging individuals to evaluate their stance on various moral and ethical issues. Potential unforeseen consequences may result in some people seeking refuge and solace in their faith, while others may find their beliefs waning, leading them toward non-belief or agnosticism.

9.1.4 Political and Social Climate as Factors for Religious and Secular Growth

The modern era has witnessed a burgeoning separation of religion from governance in several countries. Secularism is gaining prominence in tandem with the call for freedom, equality, and justice, thereby encouraging states to remain neutral in matters of religious belief. Factors like education, awareness, and individual rights have significantly contributed to this newfound advocacy for secularism.

Atheism, as an expression of secular thought and a plausible alternative to religious belief systems, has emerged as a substantial force. However, atheism's growth and widespread acceptance remains dependent on the political and social climate. Nations with a staunch separation of the state from religious institutions have facilitated the growth of atheistic thought.

Conversely, political and social environments that rigidly intertwine religion and governmental systems actively suppress or impede the atheistic narrative. In such societies, religion remains deeply ingrained in the policy-making process and societal norms, making it nearly impossible for atheism or secularism to gain a foothold.

As a global trend, the future of atheism in such regions rests on the success of secularists, humanists, and atheist communities in advocating, embracing, and promoting values of reason, evidence-based thinking, and separation of church and state.

9.1.5 Conclusion: Envisioning a Future with Atheism

The future of atheism is rooted in humanity's collective capacity to question, critique, and seek evidence-based truths, all while prioritizing the protection of basic human rights and freedoms. As globalization and multicultural exchange shape society, religion and secularism will continue to ebb and flow according to prevalent cultural, political, and social factors.

By evaluating these global trends and understanding the role of religion and secularism, we paint a crucial picture of what lies ahead for atheism. Bolstered by progressive movements, civil liberties, and scientific advancements, atheism's trajectory remains upward, albeit with its share of obstacles and challenges. Its persistence will mainly depend on the secular and atheist communities advocating for continuing moral growth, widening scientific understanding, and embracing the intrinsic potential of human beings to derive meaning, purpose, and satisfaction from their lives.

In essence, the future of atheism relies on society's willingness to adopt and foster principles of reason, skepticism, and inquiry, leading to a more coherent, tolerant, and diverse world – one where differing beliefs coexist, and atheism serves as a viable option for those seeking answers to profound existential questions.

10. Resources for the Atheist Journey: Books, Organizations, and Communities

10.1 Books for the Atheist Journey

For those who are interested in delving deeper into the philosophy of atheism and secularism, the world of literature has much to offer. Over the years, there have been countless books written on the subject, catering to various stages of understanding and levels of interest. Here, we list some of the timeless, influential books that have shaped the landscape of atheistic thought:

10.1.1 Foundational Works

1. **Why I Am Not a Christian: And Other Essays on Religion and Related Subjects** by *Bertrand Russell* Russell, a renowned philosopher and advocate of reason, cogently presents his case for why he cannot accept the tenets of Christianity or any religion. The book contains an assortment of his essays on theology, politics, morality, and more.
2. **The Age of Reason** by *Thomas Paine* Published in 1794, Paine critiques institutionalized religion and the

Bible, challenging readers to question long-held beliefs and think for themselves. It makes the case for the primacy of reason over revelation and is a classic text of Enlightenment thought.

3. **On the Nature of Things** by *Lucretius* A classical Roman philosophical epic by the poet and philosopher Lucretius, this work sets forth the principles of Epicurean philosophy and argues for a natural, materialistic understanding of the universe.

10.1.2 Contemporary Classics

1. **The God Delusion** by *Richard Dawkins* Dawkins, a respected evolutionary biologist, argues that belief in the existence of a personal God is irrational and unsupported by evidence. The book has been a best-seller and influential force in contemporary atheism.
2. **God Is Not Great: How Religion Poisons Everything** by *Christopher Hitchens* Hitchens critiques religion and its negative effects on society, using wit and fierce logic to make his case. This book highlights the dangers and absurdities of blind faith and religious dogma.
3. **The End of Faith: Religion, Terror, and the Future of Reason** by *Sam Harris* Harris examines the role of faith in our modern society and its correlation with violence and irrationality. He cogently advocates for a secular moral framework based on reason and evidence.

10.1.3 Books on Secular Morality and Ethics

1. **The Moral Landscape: How Science Can Determine Human Values** by *Sam Harris* Harris argues that our understanding of morality should be

grounded in science and reason, rather than religious dogma. He proposes an evidence-based framework for ethics that prioritizes human well-being.

2. **Humanism: An Introduction** by *Jim Herrick* A comprehensive guide to humanist thought and practice, Herrick introduces readers to the philosophical basis of humanism, its history, and its contributions to contemporary moral and ethical discussions.

10.1.4 Biographical and Autobiographical Works

1. **Infidel** by *Ayaan Hirsi Ali* Ali shares her journey from growing up in a strict Muslim family in Somalia to becoming an outspoken critic of Islam and advocate for women's rights, secularism, and free speech.

2. **Deconverted: A Journey from Religion to Reason** by *Seth Andrews* Andrews, a former Christian radio host, chronicles his path from religious belief to atheism and skepticism. The book offers insight into the challenges faced by those leaving their faith, as well as the freedom that comes with embracing reason and rationality.

10.2 Organizations for Nonbelievers

In addition to literature, various organizations exist to support atheists, agnostics, and secularists in their pursuit of a world governed by reason and evidence. These organizations champion the separation of religion and state, promote science and humanist values, and offer resources for those questioning their faith. Some examples include:

1. **American Atheists** (https://www.atheists.org/) American Atheists is a prominent national

organization that fights for the rights of atheists, works to remove the influence of religion from government, and provides a wide range of resources for the atheist community.

2. **Center for Inquiry** (https://centerforinquiry.org/) The Center for Inquiry promotes secular humanist values, critical thinking, and the scientific outlook. It operates the Committee for Skeptical Inquiry, the Council for Secular Humanism, and the Richard Dawkins Foundation for Reason and Science.

3. **Freedom From Religion Foundation** (https://ffrf.org/) FFRF is an organization dedicated to the separation of church and state, working to educate the public about nontheism and promote reason and skepticism.

10.3 Communities for Atheists

The atheist journey can be isolating, especially for those living in religious communities. Luckily, various informal and formal communities exist to help connect nonbelievers with like-minded individuals:

1. **Meetup.com Atheist Groups** Meetup is a platform for organizing and discovering local face-to-face group gatherings. Many cities have atheist, agnostic or secularist Meetup groups where you can connect with people in your area who share your beliefs.

2. **Reddit Atheism** (https://www.reddit.com/r/atheism/) An online community where atheists can discuss, ask questions, share stories, and connect with a diverse group of thinkers from around the world.

3. **Atheist Nexus** (http://www.atheistnexus.org/) A social networking site for atheists, agnostic, humanists, and other non-religious individuals to connect, share ideas, and build a supportive online community.

No matter where you are on your atheist journey, there is an abundance of resources to further explore secularism, humanism, and the philosophy of non-belief. Whether through books, organizations, or communities, you are not alone in your quest for knowledge, reason, and truth.

10. Resources for the Atheist Journey: Books, Organizations, and Communities

As you continue on your journey exploring the philosophy of non-belief, it's important to immerse yourself in the various resources that can offer guidance, support, and comradeship. This can take various forms, such as books, organizations, and communities where like-minded individuals gather to discuss, debate, and deepen their understanding of atheism and related subjects. This section delves deeper into these resources, recommending a selection of books, introducing prominent atheist organizations, and highlighting communities where you can connect with fellow atheists.

10.1 Books for the Atheist Journey

Reading is essential in understanding and strengthening one's perspective on atheism. The following books offer invaluable insights into the philosophy of non-belief, secularism, humanism, and critical thinking, and should be considered essential reading for anyone interested in atheism.

10.1.1 Classics

1. **The God Delusion** by Richard Dawkins: This book is a modern classic on atheism and critiques the concept of God from a scientific perspective. Dawkins dismantles the main arguments for God's existence and encourages readers to question religious beliefs.
2. **God is Not Great: How Religion Poisons Everything** by Christopher Hitchens: Hitchens' book is a searing criticism of organized religion and its negative influence on human history. He examines the ways in which faith has been used as a tool for oppression, violence, and intellectual stagnation.
3. **Letter to a Christian Nation** by Sam Harris: In this concise yet compelling work, Harris directly addresses Christians in the United States and challenges their specific beliefs, particularly those that contribute to public policy decisions and social attitudes.

10.1.2 Philosophy and Critical Thinking

1. **Breaking the Spell: Religion as a Natural Phenomenon** by Daniel C. Dennett: This book approaches religion from a casual, evolutionary perspective to analyze its origins and development. Dennett explores how religious beliefs have evolved over time and how they fulfill various human needs.
2. **The Demon-Haunted World: Science as a Candle in the Dark** by Carl Sagan: Sagan's work is a celebration of science and skepticism, advocating for critical thinking skills and the application of the scientific method to all aspects of life, including religion as well as superstition.

10.1.3 Humanism and Morality

1. **The Moral Landscape: How Science Can Determine Human Values** by Sam Harris: Harris argues that science, not religion, should be the basis for determining human values and morality. He explores objective and cross-cultural ethical principles and how they can be used to build a solid moral foundation.
2. **Good Without God: What a Billion Nonreligious People Do Believe** by Greg M. Epstein: This book highlights the values and practices of secular humanism as an alternative to religious belief systems. Epstein illustrates how a secular moral framework can lead to a fulfilling and enriching life.

10.2 Organizations Promoting Atheism, Secularism, and Critical Thinking

There are numerous national and international organizations that promote atheism, secularism, and critical thinking. These organizations engage in activities such as organizing conferences, providing educational resources, advocating for secular public policy, and promoting science literacy. Some prominent organizations include:

1. **American Atheists** (www.atheists.org): Founded in 1963 by Madalyn Murray O'Hair, American Atheists fights for the separation of church and state and the removal of religious influence from public policy. They also work to provide resources and support for atheists in the United States.
2. **The Richard Dawkins Foundation for Reason and Science** (www.richarddawkins.net): Launched by acclaimed evolutionary biologist and prominent

atheist Richard Dawkins, this foundation promotes scientific education, critical thinking, and a secular worldview. It produces educational materials, supports research, and engages in outreach efforts for the advancement of reason and skepticism.

3. **Freedom From Religion Foundation** (www.ffrf.org): FFRF is an American non-profit organization that works to protect the constitutional principle of the separation of church and state. They provide legal assistance to challenge religious infringements on public policy, offer educational resources, and organize events to support atheists and other nonreligious individuals.

4. **Center for Inquiry** (www.centerforinquiry.org): This organization promotes critical thinking, skepticism, secularism, and humanism through education, outreach, and advocacy. It houses a vast collection of resources, conducts research, publishes journals, and hosts conferences and events.

10.3 Communities for Atheists

There are numerous online and offline communities where atheists can connect with like-minded individuals, engage in thought-provoking discussions, attend events, and receive support. Some platforms and forums where you can find atheist communities include:

1. **Reddit** (www.reddit.com): The r/atheism subreddit is an active online community where atheists can share news, stories, and discuss various topics related to non-belief.

2. **Meetup** (www.meetup.com): Meetup has numerous atheist, secular, and humanist groups that host events and gatherings in cities around the world. Joining

these groups can help you connect with people in your local area who share your interests and beliefs.
3. **Facebook Groups**: Facebook has atheist, secular, and humanist groups where atheists can connect, discuss, and engage with like-minded individuals. Simply search for these keywords in Facebook's search bar and request to join relevant groups.
4. **Local Secular and Humanist Organizations**: Check with local secular and humanist organizations in your area to find out about gatherings, events, and meetings where you can meet others who share your perspective.

In conclusion, there is a wealth of resources available for those seeking to understand and explore atheism, secularism, and critical thinking. By engaging with these books, organizations, and communities, you will develop a strong foundation for your own journey into the philosophy of non-belief.

10. Resources for the Atheist Journey: Books, Organizations, and Communities

As you delve deeper into the world of atheism, you'll find that there are numerous resources to help you continue your journey. From thought-provoking books and influential organizations to vibrant communities, these resources can help you understand more about the philosophy of non-belief and connect with fellow atheists around the world. In this section, we'll explore some of these resources so that you can further equip yourself with knowledge, connections, and support.

Books for the Inquisitive Atheist

Books are often the first point of contact for someone exploring atheism, and they provide a wealth of knowledge and thought-provoking discussions. Some of the most influential books on the topic include:

1. *The God Delusion* by Richard Dawkins - This best-selling book is one of the most well-known atheist texts. Dawkins uses logical arguments, evidence from various fields, and a clear and witty writing style to argue against the existence of God and in favor of rational scientific inquiry.
2. *God is Not Great: How Religion Poisons Everything* by Christopher Hitchens - Hitchens presents a powerful critique of religion, detailing how it can lead to violence, oppression, and harmful falsehoods. His book is rich with historical examples and a scathing wit, making it a must-read for anyone questioning the role of faith in society.
3. *Letter to a Christian Nation* by Sam Harris - As a short and concise book, this serves as an excellent introduction to atheist arguments. Harris targets the beliefs of American Christians, presenting evidence and arguments that debunk many popular religious claims.
4. *Why I Am Not a Christian* by Bertrand Russell - This classic essay, penned by the famous philosopher and mathematician, has inspired many skeptics throughout the years. Russell examines the arguments for Christianity and finds them lacking, offering a thoughtful and inspiring defense of non-belief.
5. *Breaking the Spell: Religion as a Natural Phenomenon* by Daniel C. Dennett - This thought-provoking book takes a naturalistic approach to the

study of religion. Dennett explores why religion exists in the first place and how it has evolved over time. This book is perfect for atheists who appreciate a scientific and analytical approach to understanding faith.

Organizations Supporting Atheism and Secularism

A number of organizations around the world actively work to promote atheism, humanism, and the separation of church and state. Some of these groups include:

1. **American Atheists** - Founded by Madalyn Murray O'Hair in 1963, American Atheists is dedicated to protecting the rights of atheists and advocating for the separation of religion from government. They also organize conventions, provide resources, and offer networking opportunities for atheists. Visit their website
2. **Freedom From Religion Foundation (FFRF)** - The FFRF is a non-profit organization that focuses on promoting the constitutional principle of the separation of church and state. They also work to educate the public on matters relating to non-theism. Visit their website
3. **Secular Coalition for America** - The Secular Coalition is dedicated to advocating for secularist policies in the United States. They work to ensure that secular Americans have a voice in the political process and that their rights are protected. Visit their website
4. **Center for Inquiry (CFI)** - CFI is a nonprofit organization that works to promote reason, science, and secularism. They organize events, publish

articles, and offer educational resources to help advance their goals. Visit their website
5. **International Humanist and Ethical Union (IHEU)** - The IHEU is the global representative body for humanist organizations worldwide. They promote human rights, secularism, and humanist values, while offering a sense of community for like-minded individuals. Visit their website

Online Communities and Social Networks

Online platforms can be invaluable for atheists who want to connect with others who share similar beliefs. These communities foster discussion, support, and camaraderie for those seeking to engage with other like-minded individuals:

1. **Reddit** - Numerous atheist and secular communities can be found on Reddit, including r/atheism, r/TrueAtheism, and r/humanism. These forums allow users to discuss relevant topics, ask questions, and share experiences.
2. **Facebook Groups** - Facebook is home to many atheist and secularist groups, with some catering to specific interests or local communities. Simply search "atheist" or "secular" in the Groups section of Facebook to find a group that aligns with your interests.
3. **Meetup.com** - This website is an excellent resource for finding local atheist, humanist, or skeptic groups in your area. These groups often organize social events, discussions, and educational presentations that can provide a sense of community and support. Find local groups on Meetup
4. **Discord Communities** - Discord is a popular platform for real-time text and voice chat, and it hosts various atheist communities where members can engage in

discussions and debates, or simply relax and have friendly conversations. Find an atheist community on Discord

These resources can provide valuable support, information, and connections as you continue your atheist journey. Remember that exploration, education, and critical thinking are key aspects of any philosophical journey, and engaging with these resources can help you develop your understanding of atheism and your own personal beliefs.

Copyrights and Content Disclaimers:

AI-Assisted Content Disclaimer:
The content of this book has been generated with the assistance of artificial intelligence (AI) language models like CHatGPT and Llama. While efforts have been made to ensure the accuracy and relevance of the information provided, the author and publisher make no warranties or guarantees regarding the completeness, reliability, or suitability of the content for any specific purpose. The AI-generated content may contain errors, inaccuracies, or outdated information, and readers should exercise caution and independently verify any information before relying on it. The author and publisher shall not be held responsible for any consequences arising from the use of or reliance on the AI-generated content in this book.

General Disclaimer:
We use content-generating tools for creating this book and source a large amount of the material from text-generation tools. We make financial material and data available through our Services. In order to do so we rely on a variety of sources to gather this information. We believe these to be reliable, credible, and accurate sources. However, there may be times when the information is incorrect.
WE MAKE NO CLAIMS OR REPRESENTATIONS AS TO THE ACCURACY, COMPLETENESS, OR TRUTH OF ANY MATERIAL CONTAINED ON OUR book. NOR WILL WE BE LIABLE FOR ANY ERRORS INACCURACIES OR OMISSIONS, AND SPECIFICALLY DISCLAIMS ANY IMPLIED WARRANTIES OR MERCHANTABILITY OR FITNESS FOR ANY PARTICULAR PURPOSE AND SHALL IN NO EVENT BE LIABLE FOR ANY LOSS OF PROFIT OR ANY OTHER COMMERCIAL OR PROPERTY DAMAGE, INCLUDING BUT NOT LIMITED TO SPECIAL, INCIDENTAL, CONSEQUENTIAL, OR OTHER DAMAGES; OR FOR

DELAYS IN THE CONTENT OR TRANSMISSION OF THE DATA ON OUR book, OR THAT THE BOOK WILL ALWAYS BE AVAILABLE.

In addition to the above, it is important to note that language models like ChatGPT are based on deep learning techniques and have been trained on vast amounts of text data to generate human-like text. This text data includes a variety of sources such as books, articles, websites, and much more. This training process allows the model to learn patterns and relationships within the text and generate outputs that are coherent and contextually appropriate.

Language models like ChatGPT can be used in a variety of applications, including but not limited to, customer service, content creation, and language translation. In customer service, for example, language models can be used to answer customer inquiries quickly and accurately, freeing up human agents to handle more complex tasks. In content creation, language models can be used to generate articles, summaries, and captions, saving time and effort for content creators. In language translation, language models can assist in translating text from one language to another with high accuracy, helping to break down language barriers.

It's important to keep in mind, however, that while language models have made great strides in generating human-like text, they are not perfect. There are still limitations to the model's understanding of the context and meaning of the text, and it may generate outputs that are incorrect or offensive. As such, it's important to use language models with caution and always verify the accuracy of the outputs generated by the model.

Financial Disclaimer

This book is dedicated to helping you understand the world of online investing, removing any fears you may have about getting started and helping you choose good investments. Our goal is to help you take control of your financial well-being by delivering a solid financial education and responsible investing strategies. However, the information contained on this book and in our services is for general information and educational purposes only. It is not intended as a substitute for legal, commercial and/or financial advice from a licensed professional. The business of online investing is a complicated matter that requires serious financial due diligence for each investment in order to be successful. You are strongly advised to seek the services of qualified, competent professionals prior to engaging in any investment that may impact you finances. This information is provided by this book, including how it was made, collectively referred to as the "Services."

Be Careful With Your Money. Only use strategies that you both understand the potential risks of and are comfortable taking. It is your responsibility to invest wisely and to safeguard your personal and financial information.

We believe we have a great community of investors looking to achieve and help each other achieve financial success through investing. Accordingly we encourage people to comment on our blog and possibly in the future our forum. Many people will contribute in this matter, however, there will be times when people provide misleading, deceptive or incorrect information, unintentionally or otherwise.

You should NEVER rely upon any information or opinions you read on this book, or any book that we may link to. The information you read here and in our services should be used as a launching point for your OWN RESEARCH into various companies and investing strategies so that you can make an informed decision about where and how to invest your money.

WE DO NOT GUARANTEE THE VERACITY, RELIABILITY OR COMPLETENESS OF ANY INFORMATION PROVIDED IN THE COMMENTS, FORUM OR OTHER PUBLIC AREAS OF THE book OR IN ANY HYPERLINK APPEARING ON OUR book.

Our Services are provided to help you to understand how to make good investment and personal financial decisions for yourself. You are solely responsible for the investment decisions you make. We will not be responsible for any errors or omissions on the book including in articles or postings, for hyperlinks embedded in messages, or for any results obtained from the use of such information. Nor, will we be liable for any loss or damage, including consequential damages, if any, caused by a reader's reliance on any information obtained through the use of our Services. Please do not use our book If you do not accept self-responsibility for your actions.

The U.S. Securities and Exchange Commission, (SEC), has published additional information on Cyberfraud to help you recognize and combat it effectively. You can also get additional help about online investment schemes and how to avoid them at the following books:http://www.sec.gov and http://www.finra.org, and http://www.nasaa.org these are each organizations set-up to help protect online investors.

If you choose ignore our advice and do not do independent research of the various industries, companies, and stocks, you intend to invest in and rely solely on information, "tips," or opinions found on our book – you agree that you have made a conscious, personal decision of your own free will and will not try to hold us responsible for the results thereof under any circumstance. The Services offered herein is not for the purpose of acting as your personal investment advisor. We do not know all the relevant facts about you and/or your individual needs, and we do not represent or claim that any of our Services are suitable for your needs. You should seek a registered investment advisor if you are looking for personalized advice.

Links to Other Sites. You will also be able to link to other books from time to time, through our Site. We do not have any control over the content or actions of the books we link to and will not be liable for anything that occurs in connection with the use of such books. The inclusion of any links, unless otherwise expressly stated, should not be seen as an endorsement or recommendation of that book or the views expressed therein. You, and only you, are responsible for doing your own due diligence on any book prior to doing any business with them.

Liability Disclaimers and Limitations: Under no circumstances, including but not limited to negligence, will we, nor our partners if any, or any of our affiliates, be held responsible or liable, directly or indirectly, for any loss or damage, whatsoever arising out of, or in connection with, the use of our Services, including without limitation, direct, indirect, consequential, unexpected, special, exemplary or other damages that may result, including but not limited to economic loss, injury, illness or death or any other type of loss or damage, or unexpected or adverse reactions to suggestions contained herein or otherwise caused or alleged to have been caused to you in connection with your use of any advice, goods or services you receive on the Site, regardless of the source, or any other book that you may have visited via links from our book, even if advised of the possibility of such damages.

Applicable law may not allow the limitation or exclusion of liability or incidental or consequential damages (including but not limited to lost data), so the above limitation or exclusion may not apply to you. However, in no event shall the total liability to you by us for all damages, losses, and causes of action (whether in contract, tort, or otherwise) exceed the amount paid by you to us, if any, for the use of our Services, if any. And by using our Site you expressly agree not to try to hold us liable for any consequences that result based on your use of our Services or the information provided therein, at any time, or for any reason, regardless of the circumstances.

Specific Results Disclaimer. We are dedicated to helping you take control of your financial well-being through education and investment. We provide strategies, opinions, resources and other Services that are specifically designed to cut through the noise and hype to help you make better personal finance and investment decisions. However, there is no way to guarantee any strategy or technique to be 100% effective, as results will vary by individual, and the effort and commitment they make toward achieving their goal. And, unfortunately we don't know you. Therefore, in using and/or purchasing our services you expressly agree that the results you receive from the use of those Services are solely up to you. In addition, you also expressly agree that all risks of use and any consequences of such use shall be borne exclusively by you. And that you will not to try to hold us liable at any time, or for any reason, regardless of the circumstances.

As stipulated by law, we can not and do not make any guarantees about your ability to achieve any particular results by using any Service purchased through our book. Nothing on this page, our book, or any of our services is a promise or guarantee of results, including that you will make any particular amount of money or, any money at all, you also understand, that all investments come with some risk and you may actually lose money while investing. Accordingly, any results stated on our book, in the form of testimonials, case studies or otherwise are illustrative of concepts only and should not be considered average results, or promises for actual or future performance.

tolerance, and the ability to consistently apply the strategies and techniques discussed.

Printed in Great Britain
by Amazon

31673222R00076